# My Days and Nights
# on the Battlefield

# My Days and Nights on the Battlefield

A view of the American Civil War by
a Reporter for the Boston Journal

Charles Carleton Coffin

LEONAUR

*My Days and Nights on the Battlefield: a view of the American Civil War*
*by a Reporter for the Boston Journal*
by Charles Carleton Coffin

Leonaur is an imprint of Oakpast Ltd

Material original to this edition and
presentation of text in this form
copyright © 2009 Oakpast Ltd

ISBN: 978-1-84677-866-7 (hardcover)
ISBN: 978-1-84677-865-0 (softcover)

http://www.leonaur.com

**Publisher's Notes**

The views expressed in this book are not necessarily
those of the publisher.

# Contents

# Military Terms

*Abatis.*—Trees cut down, their branches made sharp, and used to block a road, or placed in front of fortifications.

*Advance.*—Any portion of an army which is in front of the rest.

*Aides-de-camp.*—Officers selected by general officers to assist them in their military duties.

*Ambulances.*—Carriages for the sick and wounded.

*Battery.*—A battery consists of one or more pieces of artillery. A full battery of field artillery consists of six cannon.

*Battalion.*—A battalion consists of two or more companies, but less than a regiment.

*Bombardment.*—Throwing shot or shells into a fort or earthwork.

*Canister.*—A tin cylinder filled with cast-iron shot. When the gun is fired, the cylinder bursts and scatters the shot over a wide surface of ground.

*Caisson.*—An artillery carriage, containing ammunition for immediate use.

*Casemate.*—A covered chamber in fortifications, protected by earth from shot and shells.

*Columbiad.*—A cannon, invented by Colonel Bomford, of very large calibre, used for throwing shot or shells. A ten-inch columbiad weighs 15,400 pounds, and is ten and a half feet long.

*Column.*—A position in which troops may be placed. A column *en route* is the order in which they march from one part of the country to another. A column of attack is the order in which they go into battle.

*Countersign.*—A particular word given out by the highest officer in command, entrusted to guards, pickets, and sentinels, and to those who may have occasion to pass them.

*Embrasure.*—An opening cut in embankments for the muzzles of the cannon.

*Enfilade.*—To sweep the whole length of the inside of a fortification or a line of troops.

*Field-Works.*—An embankment of earth excavated from a ditch surrounding a town or a fort.

*Flank.*—The right or left side of a body of men, or place. When it is said that the enemy by a flank march outflanked our right wing, it is understood that he put himself on our right hand. When two armies stand face to face the right flank of one is opposite the left flank of the other.

*File.*—Two soldiers,—a front rank and a rear rank man.

*Fuse.*—A slow-burning composition in shells, set on fire by the flash of the cannon. The length of the fuse is proportioned to the intended range of the shells.

*Grape.*—A large number of small balls tied up in a bag.

*Howitzer.*—A cannon of large calibre and short range, commonly used for throwing shells, grape, and canister.

*Limber.*—The fore part of a field gun-carriage, to which the horses are attached. It has two wheels, and carries ammunition the same as the caisson.

*Pontoon.*—A bridge of boats for crossing streams, which may be carried in wagons.

*Parabola.*—The curve described by a shell in the air.

*Range.*—The distance to which shot, shells, or bullets may be fired.

*Reveille.*—The first drum-beat in the morning.

*Rifle-Pits.*—Excavations in the earth or other shelter for riflemen.

*Spherical Case.*—A thin shell of cast-iron filled with bullets, with a fuse, and a charge of powder sufficient to burst it. It contains about ninety bullets.

*Wings.*—The right and left divisions of a body of troops, distinguished from the centre.

# Introduction

In my boyhood I loved to sit beside my grandfather and listen to his stories of Bunker Hill and Saratoga,—how he and his comrades stood upon those fields and fought for their country. I could almost see the fight and hear the cannon's roar, the rattle of the musketry, and the shouts of victory. They won their independence, and established the best government the world ever saw. But there are men in this country who hate that government, who have plotted against it, and who have brought about the present Great Rebellion to destroy it. I have witnessed some of the battles which have been fought during this war, although I have not been a soldier, as my grandfather was, and I shall try, in this volume, to picture those scenes, and give correct descriptions of the ground, the marching of the troops, the positions they occupied, and other things, that you may understand how your father, or your brothers, or your friends, fought for the dear old flag.

# CHAPTER 1

# How the Rebellion Came About

Many of you have seen the springs which form the trickling rivulets upon the hillsides. How small they are. You can almost drink them dry. But in the valley the silver threads become a brook, which widens to a river rolling to the far-off ocean. So is it with the ever-flowing stream of time. The things which were of small account a hundred years ago are powerful forces to-day. Great events do not usually result from one cause, but from many causes. To ascertain how the rebellion came about, let us read history.

Nearly three hundred years ago, when Elizabeth was Queen of England, Sir Walter Raleigh sailed across the Atlantic Ocean to explore the newly discovered Continent of America. Sir Walter was a sailor, a soldier, and one of the gentleman attendants of the Queen. He was so courteous and gallant that he once threw his gold-laced scarlet cloak upon the ground for a mat, that the Queen might not step her royal foot in the mud. At that time America was an unexplored wilderness. The old navigators had sailed along the coasts, but the smooth waters of the great lakes and rivers had never been ruffled by the oars of European boatmen.

Sir Walter found a beautiful land, shaded by grand old forests; also fertile fields, waving with corn and a broad-leaved plant with purple flowers, which the Indians smoked in pipes of flint and vermilion stone brought from the cliffs of the great Missouri River.

The sailors learned to smoke, and when Sir Walter returned to England they puffed their pipes in the streets. The people were amazed, and wondered if the sailors were on fire. So tobacco began to be used in England. That was in 1584. We shall see that a little tobacco-smoke whiffed nearly three hundred years ago has had an influence in bringing about the rebellion.

Twenty years rolled by. London merchants dreamed of wealth in store for them in Virginia. A company was formed to colonize the country. Many of the merchants had spendthrift sons, who were also idle and given to bad habits. These young fellows thought it degrading to work. In those Western woods across the ocean, along the great rivers and upon the blue mountains, they saw in imagination a wild, roving, reckless life. They could hunt the wild beasts. They could live without the restraints of society. They had heard wonderful stories of exhaustless mines of gold and silver. There they could get rich, and that was the land for them.

A vessel with five hundred colonists was fitted out. There were only sixteen men of the five hundred accustomed to work; the others called themselves gentlemen and cavaliers. They settled at Jamestown. They found no rich gold-mines, and wealth was not to be had on the fertile plains without labour. Not knowing how to cultivate the soil, and hating work, they had a hard time. They suffered for want of food. Many died from starvation. Yet more of the same indolent class joined the colony,—young men who had had rows with tutors at school, and who had broken the heads of London watchmen in their midnight revels. A historian of those times says that "they were fitter to breed a riot than found a colony."

The merchants, finding that a different class of men was needed to save the colony from ruin, sent over poor labouring men, who were apprenticed to their sons. Thus the idle cavaliers were kept from starvation. Instead of working themselves, they directed the poor, hardworking men, and pocketed the profits.

Smoking began to be fashionable in England. Lawyers in big wigs, ministers in black gowns, merchants seated in their counting-houses, ladies in silks and satins, all took to this habit of the North American Indians. Tobacco was in demand. Every ship from America was freighted with it. The purple-flowered plant grew luxuriantly in the fields of Virginia, and so through the labour of the poor men the indolent cavaliers became rich.

As there were no women in the colony, some of the cavaliers sent over to England and bought themselves wives, paying a hundred pounds of tobacco for a wife. Others married Indian wives.

The jails of London were crowded with thieves and vagabonds. They had committed crime and lost their freedom. To get rid of them, the magistrates sent several ship-loads to Virginia, where they were sold to the planters as servants and labourers. Thus it came to pass that there were distinct classes in the colony,—men having rights and men without rights,—men owning labour and men owing labour,—men with power and men without power,—all of which had something to do in bringing about the rebellion.

In August, 1620, a Dutch captain sailed up James River with twenty negroes on board his ship, which he had stolen from Africa. The planters purchased them, not as apprentices, but as slaves. The captain, having made a profitable voyage, sailed for Africa to steal more. Thus the African slave-trade in America began, which became the main fountain-head and grand cause of the rebellion.

The Virginia planters wanted large plantations. Some of them had influence with King James, and obtained grants of immense estates, containing thousands of acres. All the while the common people of England were learning to smoke, snuff, and chew tobacco, and across the English Channel the Dutch burghers, housewives, and farmers were learning to puff their pipes. A pound of tobacco was worth three shillings. The planters grew richer, purchased more land and more slaves, while the apprenticed men, who had no money and no means of obtaining any, of course could not become land-owners. Thus the three classes of men—planters, poor white men, and slaves—became perpetually distinct.

By the charter which the company of London merchants had received from the King, owners of land only were allowed to have a voice in the management of public affairs. They only could hold office. A poor man could not have anything to do with enacting or administering the laws. In 1705, a historian, then writing, says:

> There are men with great estates, who take care to supply the poor with goods, and who are sure to keep them always in debt, and consequently dependent. Out of this number are chosen the Council, Assembly, Justices of the Peace, and other officers, who conspire together to wield power.[1]

Thus a few rich men managed all the affairs of the colony. They were able to perpetuate their power, to hand these privileges to their sons, through successive generations.

At the present time there are many men and women in Virginia who consider themselves as belonging to the first families, because they are descendants of those who settled the country. The great estates have passed from the family name,—squandered by the disso-

---

1: Quarry.

lute and indolent sons. They are poor, but very proud, and call themselves noble-born. They look with contempt upon a man who works for a living. I saw a great estate, which was once owned by one of these proud families, near the Antietam battle-field, but spendthrift sons have squandered it, and there is but little left. The land is worn out, but the owner of the remaining acres,—poor, but priding himself upon his high birth, looking with haughty contempt upon men who work,—in the summer of 1860, day after day, was seen sitting upon his horse, with an umbrella over his head to keep off the sun, *overseeing his two negro women, who were hoeing corn!*

All of these springs which started in Virginia tinged, entered into, and gave colour to society throughout the South. There were great estates, privileged classes, a few rich and many poor men. There were planters, poor white men, and slaves.

In those old times pirates sailed the seas, plundering and destroying ships. They swarmed around the West India Islands, and sold their spoils to the people of Charleston, South Carolina. There, for several years, the freebooters refitted their ships, and had a hearty welcome. But the King's ships of war broke up the business, and commerce again had peaceful possession of the ocean.

These things gave direction to the stream, influencing the development and growth of the colonies, which became States in the Union, and which seceded in 1861.

********

While the Dutch captain was bargaining off his negroes to the planters in 1620 at Jamestown, another vessel was sailing from Plymouth harbour, in England, for a voyage across the Atlantic. Years before, in the little town of Scrooby, a man with a long white beard, by the name of Clifton, had preached what he called a pure religious doctrine. Those who went to hear him, and who believed what he preached, soon came to be called Puritans. Most of them were poor, hard-working English farmers and villagers. There was much discussion, controversy, bigotry, and bitterness in religion at that time, and these poor men were driven from county to county, till finally they were obliged to flee to Holland to escape persecution and save their lives. King James himself was one of their most bitter persecutors. He declared that he would "harry every one of them out of England." After remaining in Holland several years, they obtained permission of the King to sail for North America.

On a December morning the vessel, after five months' tossing upon the ocean, lay at anchor in the harbour of Cape Cod. Those on board had no charter of government. They were not men who had had midnight revels in London, but men who had prayers in their families night and morning, and who met for religious worship on the Sabbath. They respected law, loved order, and knew that it would be necessary to have a form of government in the colony. They assembled in the cabin of the ship, and, after prayer, signed their names to an agreement to obey all the rules, regulations, and laws which might be enacted by the majority. Then they elected a governor, each man having a voice in the election. It was what might be called the first town-meeting in America. Thus democratic liberty and Christian worship, independent of forms established by kings and bishops, had a beginning in this country.

The climate was cold, the seasons short, the soil sterile, and so the settlers of Cape Cod were obliged to work hard to obtain a living. In consequence, they and their descendants became active, industrious, and energetic. Thus they laid the foundations for thrift and enterprise. They did not look upon labour as degrading, but as ennobling. They passed laws, that men able to work should not be idle. They were not rich enough to own great estates, but each man had his own little farm. There was, therefore, no landed aristocracy, such as was growing into power in Virginia. They were not able to own labour to any great extent. There were a few apprenticed men, and some negro slaves, but the social and political influences were all different from those in the Southern colonies. The time came when apprenticed men were released from service, and the slaves set free.

These hard-working men did not wish to have their children grow up in ignorance. In order, therefore, that every child might become an intelligent citizen and member of society, they established common schools and founded colleges. In 1640, just twenty years after the landing at Plymouth, they had a printing-press at Cambridge.

The cavaliers of Virginia, instead of establishing schools, sent their sons to England to be educated, leaving the children of the poor men to grow up in ignorance. They did not want them to obtain an education. In 1670, fifty years after the Dutch captain had bartered off his negroes for tobacco,—fifty years from the election of the first governor by the people in the cabin of the Mayflower,—the King appointed Commissioners of Education, who addressed letters to the governors of the colonies upon the subject. The Governor of Connecticut replied, that one fourth of the entire income of the colony was laid out in maintaining public schools. Governor Berkeley, of Virginia, who owned a great plantation and many slaves, and who wanted to keep the government in the hands of the few privileged families, answered—

"I thank God there are no free schools nor printing in this colony, and I hope we shall not have them these hundred years."

All the Northern colonies established common schools, and liberally supported them, that every child might obtain an education. The Southern colonies, even when they became States, gave but little attention to education, and consequently the children became more ignorant than their fathers. Thus it has come to pass, that in the Northern States nearly all can read and write, while in the Southern States there are hundreds of thousands who do not know the alphabet.

In 1850 the State of Maine had 518,000 inhabitants; of these 2,134 could not read nor write, while the State of North Carolina, with a white population of 553,000, *had eighty thousand native whites, over twenty years of age, who had never attended school!*

The six New England States, with a population of 2,705,000, had in 1850 but eight thousand unable to read and write, while Virginia, North Carolina, South Carolina, Georgia, and Alabama—five States, with a population of 2,670,000 whites—*had two hundred and sixty-two thousand, over twenty years of age, unable to read a word!* In the Northern States educational facilities are rapidly increasing, while in the South they are fast diminishing. In 1857 there were 96,000 school-children in Vermont, and all but six thousand attended school. South Carolina the same year had 114,000 school-children; of these *ninety-five thousand* had no school privileges. Virginia had 414,000 school-children; *three hundred and seventy-two thousand* of them had no means of learning the alphabet!

In Missouri, in some of the counties, the school lands given by Congress have been sold, and the money distributed among the people, instead of being invested for the benefit of schools. With each generation ignorance has increased in the Southern States. It has been the design of the slaveholders to keep the poor white men in ignorance. There, neighbours are miles apart. There are vast tracts of land where the solitude is unbroken by the sounds of labour. Schools and newspapers cannot flourish. Information is given by word of mouth. Men are influenced to political action by the arguments and stories of stump-speakers, and not by reading newspapers. They vote as they are told, or as they are influenced by the stories they hear. So, when the leading conspirators were ready to bring about the rebellion, being in possession of the State governments, holding official positions, by misrepresentation, cunning, and wickedness, they were able to delude the ignorant poor men, and induce them to vote to secede from the Union.

Two thousand years ago the natives of India manufactured cloth from the fibres of the cotton-plant, which grew wild in the woods. The old historian, Herodotus, says that the trees bore fleeces as white as snow. A planter of South Carolina obtained some of the seeds, and began to cultivate the plant. In 1748 ten bags of cotton were shipped to Liverpool, but cotton-spinning had not then begun in England. In 1784 the custom-house officers at Liverpool seized eight bags which a planter had sent over, on the ground that it was not possible to raise so much in America. The manufacture of cotton goods was just then commencing in England, and cotton was in demand. The plant grew luxuriantly in the sunny fields of the South, but it was a day's work for a negro to separate the seed from a pound, and the planters despaired of making it a profitable crop.

A few years before the Liverpool custom-house officers seized the eight bags, a boy named Eli Whitney was attending school in Westboro', Massachusetts, who was destined to help the planters out of the difficulty. He made water-wheels, which plashed in the roadside brooks, and windmills, which whirled upon his father's barn. He made violins, which were the wonder and admiration of all musicians. He set up a shop, and made nails by machinery, and thus earned money through the Revolutionary War. When not more than twelve years old, he stayed at home from meeting one Sunday alone, and took his father's watch to pieces, and put it together again so nicely that it went as well as ever. It was not the proper business for Sunday, however.

When a young man, he went South to teach school. He happened to hear General Greene, the brave and noble man who had been a match for Lord Cornwallis, wish that there was a machine for cleaning cotton. He thought the matter over, went to work, and in a short time had a machine which, with some improvements, now does the work of a thousand negroes. He built it in secret, but the planters, getting wind of it, broke open his room, stole his invention, built machines of their own, and cheated him out of his property.

About this time there was a poor cotton-spinner in England who thought he could invent a machine for spinning. He sat up late nights, and thought how to have the wheels, cranks, and belts arranged. At times he was almost discouraged, but his patient, cheerful, loving wife encouraged him, and he succeeded at last in making a machine which would do the work of a thousand spinners. He named it Jenny, for his wife, who had been so patient and cheerful, though she and the children, some of the time while he was studying upon the invention, had little to eat.

The gin and the jenny made cotton cloth much cheaper than it had been. Many manufactories were built in England and in the New England States. More acres of cotton were planted in the South, and more negroes stolen from Africa. In the North, along the mill-streams, there was the click and clatter of machinery. A great many ships were needed to transport the cotton from the agricultural South to the manufactories of the commercial, industrious, trading North. The cotton crop of the South in 1784 was worth only a few hundred dollars, but the crop of 1860 was worth hundreds of millions, so great had been the increase.

This great demand for cotton affected trade and commerce the world over. The planters had princely incomes from the labour of their slaves. Some of them received $50,000 to $100,000 a year. They said that cotton was king, and ruled the world. They thought that the whole human race was dependent upon them, and that by withholding their cotton a single year they could compel the whole world to acknowledge their power. They were few in number,—about three hundred thousand in thirty millions of people. They used every means possible to extend and perpetuate their power. They saw that the Northern States were beehives of industry, and that the boys swarming from the Northern school-houses were becoming mechanics, farmers, teachers, engaging in all employments, and that knowledge as a power was getting the better of wealth.

The men of the North were settling the new States of the West, and political power in Congress was slipping from the hands of the South. To retain that power they must bring additional Slave States into the Union. They therefore demanded the right to take their slaves into new Territories. The Northern school-boys who had grown to be men, who had gone into the far West to build them homes, could not consent to see their children deprived of that which had made them men. They saw that if slavery came in, schools must go out. They saw that where slavery existed there were three distinct classes in society,—the few rich, unscrupulous, hard-hearted slaveholders, the many poor, ignorant, debased white men, and the slaves. They saw that free labour and slave labour could not exist together. They therefore rightfully resisted the extension of slavery into the Territories. But the slaveholders carried the day. The North was outvoted and obliged to yield.

The descendants of the first families of Virginia raised slaves for a living. It was degrading to labour, but a very honourable way of getting a living to raise pigs, mules, and negroes,—to sell them to the more southern States,—to sell their own sons and daughters! Their fathers purchased wives: why should they not sell their own children?

It was very profitable to raise negroes for the market, and the ministers of the South, in their pulpits on the Sabbath, said it was a Christian occupation. They expounded the Bible, and showed the benevolent designs of God in establishing slavery. It was right. It had the sanction of the Almighty. It was a Divine missionary institution.

Their political success, their great power, their wealth,—which they received through the unpaid labour of their slaves, and from selling their own sons and daughters,—developed their bad traits of character. They became proud, insolent, domineering, and ambitious. They demanded the right not only to extend slavery over all the Territories of the United States, but also the right to take their slaves into the Free States. They demanded that no one should speak or write against slavery. They secured the passage of a law by Congress enabling them to catch their runaway slaves. They demanded that the Constitution should be changed to favour the growth and extension of slavery. For many years they plotted against the government,—threatening to destroy it if they could not have what they demanded. They looked with utter contempt upon the hard-working men of the North. They determined to rule or ruin. Every Northern man living at the South was looked upon with suspicion. Some were tarred and feathered, others hung, and many were killed in cold blood! No Northern man could open his lips on that subject in the South. Men of the North could not travel there. The noble astronomer, Mitchell, the brave general who has laid down his life for his country, was surrounded by an ignorant, excited mob in Alabama, who were ready to hang him because he told them he was in favour of the Union. But Southern orators and political speakers were invited North, and listened to with respect by the thinking, reasoning people,—the pupils of the common schools.

Climate, trade, commerce, common schools, and industry have made the North different from the South; but there was nothing in these to bring on the war.

When the slaveholders saw that they had lost their power in Congress to pass laws for the extension of slavery, they determined to secede from the Union. When the North elected a President who declared himself opposed to the extension of slavery, they began the war. They stole forts, arsenals, money, steamboats,—everything they could lay their hands on belonging to government and individuals,— seceded from the Union, formed a confederacy, raised an army, and fired the first gun.

They planned a great empire, which should extend south to the Isthmus of Darien and west to the Pacific Ocean, and made slavery its cornerstone. They talked of conquering the North. They declared that the time would come when they would muster their slaves on Bunker Hill, when the labouring men of the North, "with hat in hand, should stand meekly before them, their masters."[2]

They besieged Fort Sumter, fired upon the ships sent to its relief, bombarded the fort and captured it. To save their country, their government, all that was dear to them, to protect their insulted, time-honoured flag, the men of the North took up arms.

2: *Richmond Enquirer.*

CHAPTER 2

# The Gathering of a Great Army

The Rebels began the war by firing upon Fort Sumter. You remember how stupefying the news of its surrender. You could not at first believe that they would fire upon the Stars and Stripes,—the flag respected and honoured everywhere on earth. When there was no longer a doubt that they had begun hostilities, you could not have felt worse if you had heard of the death of a very dear friend. But as you thought it over and reflected upon the wickedness of the act, so deliberate and terrible, you felt that you would like to see the traitors hung; not that it would be a pleasure to see men die a felon's death, but because you loved your country and its flag, with its heaven-born hues, its azure field of stars! Not that the flag is anything in itself to be protected, honoured, and revered, but because it is the emblem of constitutional liberty and freedom, the ensign of the best, freest, noblest government ever established. It had cost suffering and blood. Kings, aristocrats, despots, and tyrants, in the Old World and in the New hated it, but millions of men in other lands, suffering, abused, robbed of their rights, beheld it as their banner of hope. When you thought how it had been struck down by traitors, when you heard that the President had called for seventy five thousand troops, you hurrahed with all your might, and wished that you were old enough and big enough to go and fight the Rebels.

The drums beat in the street. You saw the soldiers hasten to take their places in the gathering ranks. You marched beside them and kept step with the music. The sunlight gleamed from their bayonets. Their standards waved in the breeze, while the drum, the fife, the bugle, and the trumpet thrilled you as never before. You marched proudly and defiantly. You felt that you could annihilate the stoutest Rebel. You followed the soldiers to the railroad depot and hurrahed till the train which bore them away was out of sight.

Let us follow them to Washington, and see the gathering of a great army. The Rebels have threatened to capture that city and make it their seat of government, and it must be saved.

We have been a quiet, peaceable nation, and have had no great standing armies of a half-million men. We know but little about war. The Northern States are unprepared for war. President Buchanan's Secretary of War, Floyd, has proved himself a thief. He has stolen several hundred thousands of muskets, thousands of pieces of artillery, sending them from the Northern arsenals to the South. The slaveholders have been for many years plotting the rebellion. They are armed, and we are not. Their arsenals are well filled, while ours are empty, because President Buchanan was a weak old man, and kept thieves and traitors in places of trust and power.

At the call of the President every village sends its soldiers, every town its company. When you listened to the soul-thrilling music of the band, and watched the long, winding train as it vanished with the troops in the distance, you had one little glimpse of the machinery of war, as when riding past a great manufactory you see a single pulley, or a row of spindles through a window. You do not see the thousands of wheels, belts, shafts,—the hundred thousand spindles, the arms of iron, fingers of brass, and springs of steel, and the mighty wheel which gives motion to all,—and so you have not seen the great, complicated, far-reaching, and powerful machinery of war.

But there is activity everywhere. Drums are beating, men assembling, soldiers marching, and hastening on in regiments. They go into camp and sleep on the ground, wrapped in their blankets. It is a new life. They have no napkins, no table-cloths at breakfast, dinner, or supper, no china plates or silver forks. Each soldier has his tin plate and cup, and makes a hearty meal of beef and bread. It is hard-baked bread. They call it *hard-tack*, because it might be tacked upon the roof of a house instead of shingles. They also have Cincinnati *chicken*. At home they called it pork; fowls are scarce and pork is plenty in camp, so they make believe it is chicken!

There is drilling by squads, companies, battalions, and by regiments. Some stand guard around the camp by day, and others go out on picket at night, to watch for the enemy. It is military life. Everything is done by orders. When you become a soldier, you cannot go and come as you please. Privates, lieutenants, captains, colonels, generals, all are subject to the orders of their superior officers. All must obey the general in command. You march, drill, eat, sleep, go to bed, and get up by order. At sunrise you hear the reveille, and at nine o'clock in the evening the tattoo. Then the candle, which has been burning in your tent with a bayonet for a candlestick, must be put out. In the dead of night, while sleeping soundly and dreaming of home, you hear the drum-beat. It is the long roll. There is a rattle of musketry. The pickets are at it. Every man springs to his feet.

"Turn out! turn out!" shouts the colonel.

"Fall in! fall in!" cries the captain.

There is confusion throughout the camp,—a trampling of feet and loud, hurried talking. In your haste you get your boots on wrong, and buckle your cartridge-box on bottom up. You rush out in the darkness, not minding your steps, and are caught by the tent-ropes. You tumble headlong, upsetting to-morrow's breakfast of beans. You take your place in the ranks, nervous, excited, and trembling at you know not what. The regiment rushes toward the firing, which suddenly ceases. An officer rides up in the darkness and says it is a false alarm! You march back to camp, cool and collected now, grumbling at the stupidity of the picket, who saw a bush, thought it was a Rebel, fired his gun, and alarmed the whole camp.

In the autumn of 1861 the army of the Potomac, encamped around Washington, numbered about two hundred thousand men. Before it marches to the battle-field, let us see how it is organized, how it looks, how it is fed; let us get an insight into its machinery.

Go up in the balloon which you see hanging in the air across the Potomac from Georgetown, and look down upon this great army. All the country round is dotted with white tents,—some in the open fields, and some half hid by the forest-trees. Looking away to the northwest you see the right wing. Arlington is the centre, and at Alexandria is the left wing. You see men in ranks, in files, in long lines, in masses, moving to and fro, marching and countermarching, learning how to fight a battle. There are thousands of wagons and horses; there are from two to three hundred pieces of artillery. How long the line, if all were on the march! Men marching in files are about three feet apart. A wagon with four horses occupies fifty feet. If this army was moving on a narrow country road, four cavalrymen riding abreast, and men in files of four, with all the artillery, ammunition-wagons, supply-trains, ambulances, and equipment, it would reach from Boston to Hartford, or from New York city to Albany, a hundred and fifty miles!

To move such a multitude, to bring order out of confusion, there must be a system, a plan, and an organization. Regiments are therefore formed into brigades, with usually about four regiments to a brigade. Three or four brigades compose a division, and three or four divisions make an army corps. A corps when full numbers from twenty-five to thirty thousand men.

When an army moves, the general commanding it issues his orders to the generals commanding the corps; they issue their orders to the division commanders, the division commanders to the brigadiers, they to the colonels, and the colonels to captains, and the captains to the companies. As the great wheel in the factory turns all the machinery, so one mind moves the whole army. The general-in-chief must designate the road which each corps shall take, the time when they are to march, where they are to march to, and sometimes the hour when they must arrive at an appointed place. The corps commanders must direct which of their divisions shall march first, what roads they shall take, and where they shall encamp at night. The division commanders direct what brigades shall march first. No corps, division, or brigade commander can take any other road than that assigned him, without producing confusion and delay.

The army must have its food regularly. Think how much food it takes to supply the city of Boston, or Cincinnati every day. Yet here are as many men as there are people in those cities. There are a great many more horses in the army than in the stables of both of those cities. All must be fed. There must be a constant supply of beef, pork, bread, beans, vinegar, sugar, and coffee, oats, corn, and hay.

The army must also have its supplies of clothing, its boots, shoes, and coats. It must have its ammunition, its millions of cartridges of different kinds; for there are a great many kinds of guns in the regiments,—Springfield and Enfield muskets, French, Belgian, Prussian, and Austrian guns, requiring a great many different kinds of ammunition. There are a great many different kinds of cannon. There must be no lack of ammunition, no mistake in its distribution. So there is the Quartermaster's Department, the Commissary, and the Ordnance Department. The Quartermaster moves and clothes the army, the Commissary feeds it, and the Ordnance officer supplies it with ammunition. The general-in-chief has a Quartermaster-General, a chief Commissary and a chief Ordnance officer, who issue their orders to the chief officers in their departments attached to each corps. They issue their orders to their subordinates in the divisions, and the division officers to those in the brigades.

Then there is a Surgeon-General, who directs all the hospital operations, who must see that the sick and wounded are all taken care of. There are camp surgeons, division, brigade, and regimental surgeons. There are hospital nurses, ambulance drivers, all subject to the orders of the surgeon. No other officer can direct them. Each department is complete in itself.

It has cost a great deal of thought, labour, and money to construct this great machinery. In creating it there has been much thinking, energy, determination, and labour; and there must be constant forethought in anticipating future wants, necessities, and contingencies, when to move, where, and how. The army does not exist of its own accord, but by constant, unremitting effort.

The people of the country determined that the Constitution, the Union, and the government bequeathed by their fathers should be preserved. They authorized the President to raise a great army. Congress voted money and men. The President, acting as the agent of the people, and as Commander-in-Chief, appointed men to bring all the materials together and organize the army. Look at what was wanted to build this mighty machine and to keep it going.

First, the hundreds of thousands of men; the thousands of horses; the thousands of barrels of beef, pork, and flour; thousands of hogsheads of sugar, vinegar, rice, salt, bags of coffee, and immense stores of other things. Thousands of tons of hay, bags of oats and corn. What numbers of men and women have been at work to get each soldier ready for the field. He has boots, clothes, and equipments. The tanner, currier, shoemaker, the manufacturer, with his swift-flying shuttles, the operator tending his looms and spinning-jennies, the tailor with his sewing-machines, the gunsmith, the harness-maker, the blacksmith,—all trades and occupations have been employed. There are saddles, bridles, knapsacks, canteens, dippers, plates, knives, stoves, kettles, tents, blankets, medicines, drums, swords, pistols, guns, cannon, powder, percussion-caps, bullets, shot, shells, wagons,--everything.

Walk leisurely through the camps, and observe the little things and the great things, see the men on the march. Then go into the Army and Navy Departments in Washington, in those brick buildings west of the President's house. In those rooms are surveys, maps, plans, papers, charts of the ocean, of the sea-coast, currents, sand-bars, shoals, the rising and falling of tides. In the Topographical Bureau you see maps of all sections of the country. There is the Ordnance Bureau, with all sorts of guns, rifles, muskets, carbines, pistols, swords, shells, rifled shot, fuses which the inventors have brought in. There are a great

25

many bureaus, with immense piles of papers and volumes, containing experiments upon the strength of iron, the trials of cannon, guns, mortars, and powder. There have been experiments to determine how much powder shall be used, whether it shall be as fine as mustard-seed or as coarse as lumps of sugar, and the results are all noted here. All the appliances of science, industry, and art are brought into use to make it the best army the world ever saw.

It is the business of the government to bring the materials together, and the business of the generals to organize it into brigades, divisions, and corps,—to determine the number of cavalry and batteries of artillery, to place weak materials in their proper places, and the strongest where they will be most needed.

The general commanding must have a plan of operations. Napoleon said that war is like a game of chess, and that a commander must make his game. He must think it out beforehand, and in such a manner that the enemy will be compelled to play it in his way and be defeated. The general-in-chief must see the end from the beginning, just as Napoleon, sticking his map of Europe full of pins, decided that he could defeat the Austrians at Austerlitz, the Prussians at Jena. That is genius. The general-in-chief makes his plan on the supposition that all his orders will be obeyed promptly, that no one will shirk responsibility, that not one of all the vast multitude will fail to do his duty.

The night before the battle of Waterloo, Napoleon sent an order to an officer to take possession of a little hillock, on which stood a farmhouse overlooking the plain. The officer thought it would do just as well if he let it go till morning, but in the morning the English had possession of the spot, and in consequence of that officer's neglect Napoleon probably lost the great battle, his army, and his empire. Great events often hang on little things, and in military operations it is of the utmost importance that they should be attended to.

From the beginning to the end, unless every man does his duty, from the general in command to the private in the ranks, there is danger of failure.

Thus the army is organized, and thus through organization it becomes a disciplined body. Instead of being a confused mass of men, horses, mules, cannon, caissons, wagons, and ambulances, it is a body which can be divided, subdivided, separated by miles of country, hurried here and there, hurled upon the enemy, and brought together again by the stroke of a pen, by a word, or the click of the telegraph.

When a battle is to be fought, the general-in-chief must not only have his plan how to get the great mass of men to the field, but he must have a plan of movement on the field. Each corps must have its position assigned. There must be a line of battle. It is not a continuous line of men, but there are wide spaces, perhaps miles wide, between the corps, divisions, and brigades. Hills, ravines, streams, swamps, houses, villages, bushes, a fence, rocks, wheat-fields, sunlight and shade, all must be taken into account. Batteries must be placed on hills, or in commanding positions to sweep all the country round. Infantry must be gathered in masses in the centre or on either wing, or deployed and separated according to circumstances. They must be sheltered. They must be thrown here or there, as they may be needed to hold or to crush the enemy. They are to stand still and be ploughed through by shot and shell, or rush into the thickest of the fight, just as they may be ordered. They are not to question the order—

*Theirs not to make reply,*
*Theirs not to reason why,*
*Theirs but to do and die.*

There are sleepless nights in the tent of the general-in-chief. When all others except the pickets are asleep, he is examining maps and plans, calculating distances, estimating the strength of his army, and asking himself whether it will do to attack the enemy, or whether he shall stand on the defensive? can this brigade be relied upon for a desperate charge? will that division hold the enemy in check? At such times, the good name, the valour, the bravery of the troops and of the officers who command them is reviewed. He weighs character. He knows who are reliable and who inefficient. He studies, examines papers, consults reports, makes calculations, sits abstractedly, walks nervously, and lies down to dream it all over again and again.

The welfare of the country, thousands of lives, and perhaps the destiny of the nation, is in his hands. How shall he arrange his corps? ought the troops to be massed in the centre, or shall he concentrate them on the wings? shall he feel of the enemy with a division or two, or rush upon him like an avalanche? Can the enemy outflank him, or get upon his rear? What if the Rebels should pounce upon his ammunition and supply-trains? What is the position of the enemy? How large is his force? How many batteries has he? How much cavalry? What do the scouts report? Are the scouts to be believed? One says the enemy is retreating, another that he is advancing. What are the probabilities? A thousand questions arise which must be answered. The prospect of success must be carefully calculated. Human life must be thrown remorselessly into the scale. All the sorrows and the tears of wives, mothers, fathers, brothers, and sisters far away, who will mourn for the dead, must be forgotten. He must shut up all tender thoughts, and become an iron man. Ah! it is not so fine a thing to be a general, perhaps, as you have imagined!

It is an incomplete, imperfect, and unsatisfactory look which you have taken of the machinery of a great army. But you can see that a very small thing may upset the best-laid plan of any commander. The cowardice of a regiment, the failure of an officer to do his duty, to be at a place at an appointed moment, the miscarriage of orders, a hundred things which you can think of, may turn a victory into a defeat. You can see that a great battle must be a grand and terrible affair; but though you may use all your powers of imagination in endeavouring to picture the positions of the troops,—how they look, how they act, how they stand amid the terrible storm, braying death, how they rush into the thickest fire, how they fall like the sere leaves of autumn,— you will fail in your conceptions of the conflict. You must see it, and be in it, to know what it is.

# CHAPTER 3

# The Battle of Bull Run

The first great battle of the war was fought near Bull Run, in Virginia. There had been skirmishing along the Potomac, in Western Virginia, and Missouri; but upon the banks of this winding stream was fought a battle which will be forever memorable. The Rebels call it the battle of Manassas. It has been called also the battle of Stone Bridge and the battle of Warrenton Road.

Bull Run is a lazy, sluggish stream, a branch of the Occoquan River, which empties into the Potomac. It rises among the Bull Run Mountains, and flows southeast through Fairfax County. Just beyond the stream, as you go west from Washington, are the plains of Manassas,— level lands, which years ago waved with corn and tobacco, but the fields long since were worn out by the thriftless farming of the slaveholders, and now they are overgrown with thickets of pine and oak.

Two railroads meet upon the plains, one running northwest through the mountain gaps into the valley of the Shenandoah, and the other running from Alexandria to Richmond, Culpepper, and the Southwest. The junction, therefore, became an important place for Rebel military operations. There, in June, 1861, General Beauregard mustered his army, which was to defeat the Union army and capture Washington. The Richmond newspapers said that this army would not only capture Washington, but would also dictate terms of peace on the banks of the Hudson. Hot-headed men, who seemed to have lost their reason through the influence of slavery and secession, thought that the Southern troops were invincible. They were confident that one Southerner could whip five Yankees. Ladies cheered them, called them chivalrous sons of the South, and urged them on to the field.

But General Beauregard, instead of advancing upon Washington, awaited an attack from the Union army, making Bull Run his line of defence, throwing up breastworks, cutting down trees, and sheltering his men beneath the thick growth of the evergreen pines.

The army of the Union, called the Army of the Potomac, assembled at Arlington Heights and Alexandria. General McDowell was placed in command. Half of his soldiers were men who had enlisted for three months, who had suddenly left their homes at the call of the President. Their term of service had nearly expired. The three years' men had been but a few days in camp. Military duties were new. They knew nothing of discipline, but they confidently expected to defeat the enemy and move on to Richmond. Few people thought of the possibility of defeat.

Let us walk up the valley of Bull Run and notice its fords, its wooded banks, the scattered farm-houses, and fields of waving grain. Ten miles from the Occoquan we come to the railroad bridge. A mile farther up is McLean's Ford; another mile carries us to Blackburn's, and another mile brings us to Mitchell's. Above these are Island Ford, Lewis Ford, and Ball's Ford. Three miles above Mitchell's there is a stone bridge, where the turnpike leading from Centreville to Warrenton crosses the stream. Two miles farther up is a place called Sudley Springs,—a cluster of houses, a little stone church, a blacksmith's shop. The stream there has dwindled to a brook, and gurgles over a rocky bed.

Going back to the stone bridge, and standing upon its parapet, you may look east to Centreville, about four miles distant, beautifully situated on a high ridge of land, but a very old, dilapidated place when you get to it. Going west from the bridge, you see upon your right hand a swell of land, and another at your left hand, south of the turnpike. A brook trickles by the roadside. Leaving the turnpike, and ascending the ridge on the north side, you see that towards Sudley Springs there are other swells of land, with wheat-fields, fences, scattered trees, and groves of pines and oaks. Looking across to the hill south of the turnpike, a half-mile distant, you see the house of Mr. Lewis, and west of it Mrs. Henry's, on the highest knoll. Mrs. Henry is an old lady, so far advanced in life that she is helpless. Going up the turnpike a mile from the bridge, you come to the toll-gate, kept by Mr. Mathey. A cross-road comes down from Sudley Springs, and leads south towards Manassas Junction, six miles distant. Leave the turnpike once more, and go northwest a half-mile, and you come to the farm of Mr. Dogan. There are farm-sheds and haystacks near his house.

This ground, from Dogan's to the ridge east of the toll-gate, across the turnpike and the trickling brook to Mr. Lewis's and Mrs. Henry's, is the battle-field. You see it,—the ridges of land, the houses, haystacks, fences, knolls, ravines, wheat-fields, turnpike, and groves of oak and pine,—a territory about two miles square.

On Saturday, June 20th, General Johnston, with nearly all the Rebel army of the Shenandoah, arrived at Manassas. Being General Beauregard's superior officer, he took command of all the troops. He had about thirty thousand men.

On Thursday, General Richardson's brigade of General McDowell's army had a skirmish with General Longstreet's brigade at Blackburn's Ford, which the Rebels call the battle of Bull Run, while that which was fought on the 21st they call the battle of Manassas. General Beauregard expected that the attack would be renewed along the fords, and posted his men accordingly.

Going down to the railroad bridge, we see General Ewell's brigade of the Rebel army on the western bank guarding the crossing. General Jones's brigade is at McLean's Ford. At Blackburn's Ford is General Longstreet's, and at Mitchell's Ford is General Bonham's. Near by Bonham's is General Earley's, General Bartow's, and General Holmes's. General Jackson's is in rear of General Bonham's. At Island Ford is General Bee and Colonel Hampton's legion, also Stuart's cavalry. At Ball's Ford is General Cocke's brigade. Above, at the Stone Bridge, is the extreme left of the Rebel army, General Evans's brigade. General Elzey's brigade of the Shenandoah army is on its way in the cars, and is expected to reach the battle-field before the contest closes. General Johnston has between fifty and sixty pieces of artillery and about one thousand cavalry.

General McDowell had also about thirty thousand men and forty-nine pieces of artillery. His army was in four divisions,—General Tyler's, General Hunter's, General Heintzelman's, and General Miles's. One brigade of General Tyler's and General Miles's division was left at Centreville to make a feint of attacking the enemy at Blackburn's and Mitchell's Fords, and to protect the rear of the army from an attack by Generals Ewell and Jones. The other divisions of the army—five brigades, numbering eighteen thousand men, with thirty-six cannon—marched soon after midnight, to be ready to make the attack by sunrise on Sunday morning.

General Tyler, with General Keyes's brigade, General Sherman's, and General Schenck's, marched down the turnpike towards the Stone Bridge, where General Evans was on the watch. General Tyler had twelve pieces of artillery,—two batteries, commanded by Ayer and Carlisle.

It is sunrise as they approach the bridge,—a calm, peaceful Sabbath morning. The troops leave the turnpike, march into a cornfield, and ascend a hill overlooking the bridge. As you stand there amid the tasselled stalks, you see the stream rippling beneath the stone arches, and upon the other bank breastworks of earth and fallen trees. Half hid beneath the oaks and pines are the Rebel regiments, their gun-barrels and bayonets flashing in the morning light. Beyond the breastworks upon the knolls are the farm-houses of Mr. Lewis and Mrs. Henry.

Captain Ayer, who has seen fighting in Mexico, brings his guns upon the hill, wheels them into position, and sights them towards the breastworks. There is a flash, a puff of smoke, a screaming in the air, and then across the stream a handful of cloud bursts into view above the Rebel lines. The shell has exploded. There is a sudden movement of the Rebel troops. It is the first gun of the morning. And now, two miles down the Run, by Mitchell's Ford, rolling, echoing, and reverberating through the forests, are other thunderings. General Richardson has been waiting impatiently to hear the signal gun. He is to make a feint of attacking. His cannonade is to begin furiously. He has six guns, and all of them are in position, throwing solid shot and shells into the wood where Longstreet's men are lying.

All of Ayer's guns are in play, hurling rifled shot and shells, which scream like an unseen demon as they fly over the cornfield, over the meadow lands, to the woods and fields beyond the stream.

General Hunter and General Heintzelman, with their divisions, have left the turnpike two miles from Centreville, at Cub Run bridge, a rickety, wooden structure, which creaks and trembles as the heavy cannon rumble over. They march into the northwest, along a narrow road,—a round-about way to Sudley Springs. It is a long march. They started at two o'clock, and have had no breakfast. They waited three hours at Cub Run, while General Tyler's division was crossing, and they are therefore three hours behind the appointed time. General McDowell calculated and intended to have them at Sudley Springs by six o'clock, but now it is nine. They stop a half-hour at the river-crossing to fill their canteens from the gurgling stream.

Looking south from the little stone church, you see clouds of dust floating over the forest-trees. The Rebels have discovered the movement, and are marching in hot haste to resist the impending attack. General Evans has left a portion of his command at Stone Bridge, and is hastening with the remainder to the second ridge of land north of the turnpike. He plants his artillery on the hill, and secretes his infantry in a thicket of pines. General Bee is on the march, so is General Bartow and General Jackson, all upon the double-quick. Rebel officers ride furiously, and shout their orders. The artillerymen lash their horses to a run. The infantry are also upon the run, sweating and panting in the hot sunshine. The noise and confusion increase. The booming deepens along the valley, for still farther down, by Blackburn's Ford, Hunt's battery is pouring its fire upon Longstreet's, Jones's, and Ewell's men.

The Union troops at Sudley Springs move across the stream. General Burnside's brigade is in advance. The Second Rhode Island infantry is thrown out, deployed as skirmishers. The men are five paces apart. They move slowly, cautiously, and nervously through the fields and thickets.

Suddenly, from bushes, trees, and fences there is a rattle of musketry. General Evans's skirmishers are firing. There are jets of flame and smoke, and a strange humming in the air. There is another rattle, a roll, a volley. The cannon join. The first great battle has begun. General Hunter hastens to the spot, and is wounded almost at the first volley, and compelled to leave the field. The contest suddenly grows fierce. The Rhode Island boys push on to closer quarters, and the Rebels under General Evans give way from a thicket to a fence, from a fence to a knoll.

General Bee arrives with his brigade to help General Evans. You see him swing up into line west of Evans, towards the haystacks by Dogan's house. He is in such a position that he can pour a fire upon the flank of the Rhode Island boys, who are pushing Evans. It is a galling fire, and the brave fellows are cut down by the raking shots from the haystacks. They are almost overwhelmed. But help is at hand. The Seventy-first New York, the Second New Hampshire, and the First Rhode Island, all belonging to Burnside's brigade, move toward the haystacks. They bring their guns to a level, and the rattle and roll begin. There are jets of flame, long lines of light, white clouds, unfolding and expanding, rolling over and over, and rising above the tree-tops. Wilder the uproar. Men fall, tossing their arms; some leap into the air, some plunge headlong, falling like logs of wood or lumps of lead. Some reel, stagger, and tumble; others lie down gently as to a night's repose, unheeding the din, commotion, and uproar. They are bleeding, torn, and mangled. Legs, arms, bodies, are crushed. They see nothing. They cannot tell what has happened. The air is full of fearful noises. An unseen storm sweeps by. The trees are splintered, crushed, and broken as if smitten by thunderbolts. Twigs and leaves fall to the ground. There is smoke, dust, wild talking, shouting, hissings, howlings, explosions. It is a new, strange, unanticipated experience to the soldiers of both armies, far different from what they thought it would be.

Far away, church-bells are tolling the hour of Sabbath worship, and children are singing sweet songs in many a Sunday school. Strange and terrible the contrast! You cannot bear to look upon the dreadful scene. How horrible those wounds! The ground is crimson with blood. You are ready to turn away, and shut the scene forever from your sight. But the battle must go on, and the war must go on till the wicked men who began it are crushed, till the honour of the dear old flag is vindicated, till the Union is restored, till the country is saved, till the slaveholder is deprived of his power, and till freedom comes to the slave. It is terrible to see, but you remember that the greatest blessing the world ever received was purchased by blood,—the blood of the Son of God. It is terrible to see, but there are worse things than war. It is worse to have the rights of men trampled in the dust; worse to have your country destroyed, to have justice, truth, and honour violated. You had better be killed, torn to pieces by cannon-shot, than lose your manhood, or yield that which makes you a man. It is better to die than give up that rich inheritance bequeathed us by our fathers, and purchased by their blood.

The battle goes on. General Porter's brigade comes to the aid of Burnside, moving towards Dogan's house. Jackson's Rebel brigade is there to meet him. Arnold's battery is in play,—guns pouring a constant stream of shot and shells upon the Rebel line. The Washington Artillery, from New Orleans, is replying from the hill south of Dogan's. Other Rebel batteries are cutting Burnside's brigade to pieces. The men are all but ready to fall back before the terrible storm. Burnside sends to Porter for help,—he asks for the brave old soldiers, the regulars, who have been true to the flag of their country, while many of their former officers have been false. They have been long in the service, and have had many fierce contests with the Indians on the Western plains. They are as true as steel. Captain Sykes commands them. He leads the way. You see them, with steady ranks, in the edge of the woods east of Dogan's house. They have been facing southwest, and now they turn to the southeast. They pass through the grove of pines, and enter the open field. They are cut through and through with solid shot, shells burst around them, men drop from the ranks, but the battalion does not falter. It sweeps on close up to the cloud of flame and smoke rolling from the hill north of the turnpike. Their muskets come to a level. There is a click, click, click, along the line. A broad sheet of flame, a white, sulphurous cloud, a deep roll like the angry growl of thunder. There is sudden staggering in the Rebel ranks. Men whirl round, and drop upon the ground. The line wavers, and breaks. They run down the hill, across the hollows, to another knoll. There they rally, and hold their ground a while. Hampton's legion and Cocke's brigade come to their support. Fugitives are brought back by the officers, who ride furiously over the field. There is a lull, and then the strife goes on, a rattling fire of musketry, and a continual booming of the cannonade.

General Heintzelman's division was in rear of General Hunter's on the march. When the battle begun the troops were several miles from Sudley Church. They were parched with thirst, and when they reached the stream they, too, stopped and filled their canteens. Burnside's and Porter's brigades were engaged two hours before Heintzelman's division reached the field. Eight regiments had driven the Rebels from their first position.

General Heintzelman marched upon the Rebels west of Dogan's house. The Rebel batteries were on a knoll, a short distance from the toll-gate. Griffin and Ricketts opened upon them with their rifled guns. Then came a great puff of smoke. It was a Rebel caisson blown up by one of Griffin's shells. It was a continuous, steady artillery fire. The gunners of the Rebel batteries were swept away by the unerring aim of Griffin's gunners. They changed position again and again, to avoid the shot. Mingled with the constant crashing of the cannonade was an irregular firing of muskets, like the pattering of rain-drops upon a roof. At times there was a quicker rattle, and heavy rolls, like the fall of a great building.

General Wilcox swung his brigade round upon Jackson's flank. The Rebel general must retreat or be cut off, and he fell back to the toll-gate, to the turnpike, across it, in confusion, to the ridge by Mrs. Henry's. Evans's, Bee's, Bartow's, and Cocke's brigades, which have been trying to hold their ground against Burnside and Porter's brigades, by this movement are also forced back to Mr. Lewis's house. The Rebels do not all go back. There are hundreds who rushed up in hot haste in the morning lying bleeding, torn, mangled, upon the wooded slopes. Some are prisoners.

I talked with a soldier of one of the Virginia regiments. We were near the Stone Bridge. He was a tall, athletic young man, dressed in a gray uniform trimmed with yellow braid.

"How many soldiers have you on the field?" I asked.

"Ninety thousand."

"Hardly that number, I guess."

"Yes, sir. We have got Beauregard's and Johnston's armies. Johnston came yesterday and a whole lot more from Richmond. If you whip us to-day, you will whip nigh to a hundred thousand."

"Who is in command?"

"Jeff Davis."

"I thought Beauregard was in command."

"Well, he was; but Jeff Davis is on the field now. I know it; for I saw him just before I was captured. He was on a white horse."

While talking, a shell screamed over our heads and fell in the woods. The Rebel batteries had opened again upon our position. Another came, and we were compelled to leave the spot.

The prisoner may have been honest in his statements. It requires much judgment to correctly estimate large armies. He was correct in saying that Jeff Davis was there. He was on the ground, watching the progress of the battle, but taking no part. He arrived in season to see the close of the contest.

After Burnside and Porter had driven Evans, Bee, and Bartow across the turnpike, General Sherman and General Keyes crossed Bull Run above the Stone Bridge and moved straight down the stream. Schenck's brigade and Ayer's and Carlisle's batteries were left to guard the rear.

Perhaps you had a brother or a father in the Second New Hampshire, or in the Seventy-first New York, or in some other regiment; or perhaps when the war is over you may wish to visit the spot and behold the ground where the first great battle was fought. You will wish to see just where they stood. Looking, then, along the line at one o'clock, you see nearest the stream General Keyes's brigade, composed of the First, Second, and Third Connecticut regiments and the Fourth Maine. Next is Sherman's brigade, composed of the Sixty-ninth and Seventy-ninth New York Militia, the Thirteenth New York Volunteers, and the Second Wisconsin. Between these and the toll-gate you see first, as you go west, Burnside's brigade, composed of the First and Second Rhode Island, the Seventy-first New York Militia, and the Second New Hampshire, and the Second Rhode Island battery; extending to the toll-house is Porter's brigade. He has Sykes's battalion of regulars, and the Eighth and Fourteenth regiments of New York Militia and Arnold's battery. Crossing the road which comes down from Sudley Springs, you see General Franklin's brigade, containing the Fifth Massachusetts Militia, the First Minnesota Volunteers, and the Fourth Pennsylvania Militia. Next you come to the men from Maine and Vermont, the Second, Fourth, and Fifth Maine, and the Second Vermont, General Howard's brigade. Beyond, upon the extreme right, is General Wilcox with the First Michigan and the Eleventh New York. Griffin's and Rickett's batteries are near at hand. There are twenty-four regiments and twenty-four pieces of artillery. There are two companies of cavalry. If we step over to the house of Mr. Lewis, we shall find General Johnston and General Beauregard in anxious consultation. General Johnston has sent officers in hot haste for reinforcements. Brigades are arriving out of breath,— General Cocke's, Holmes's, Longstreet's, Earley's. Broken regiments, fragments of companies, and stragglers are collected and brought into line. General Bonham's brigade is sent for. All but General Ewell's and General Jones's; they are left to prevent General Miles from crossing at Blackburn's Ford and attacking the Rebel army in the rear. General Johnston feels that it is a critical moment. He has been driven nearly two miles. His flank has been turned. His loss has been very great, and his troops are beginning to be disheartened. They have changed their opinions of the Yankees.

General Johnston has Barley's brigade, composed of the Seventh and Twenty-fourth Virginia, and the Seventh Louisiana; Jackson's brigade, composed of the Second, Fourth, Fifth, Twenty-seventh, and Thirty-third Virginia, and the Thirteenth Mississippi; Bee's and Bartow's brigades united, composed of two companies of the Eleventh Mississippi, Second Mississippi, First Alabama, Seventh and Eighth Georgia; Cocke's brigade, the Eighteenth, Nineteenth, and Twenty-eighth Virginia, seven companies of the Eighth, and three of the Forty-ninth Virginia; Evans's brigade, composed of Hampton's legion, Fourth South Carolina, and Wheat's Louisiana battalion; Holmes's brigade, composed of two regiments of Virginia infantry, the First Arkansas, and the Second Tennessee. Two regiments of Bonham's brigade, and Elzey's brigade were brought in before the conflict was over. Putting the detached companies into regiments, Johnston's whole force engaged in this last struggle is thirty-five regiments of infantry, and about forty pieces of artillery, all gathered upon the ridge by Mr. Lewis's and Mrs. Henry's.

There is marching to and fro of regiments. There is not much order. Regiments are scattered. The lines are not even. This is the first battle, and officers and men are inexperienced. There are a great many stragglers on both sides; more, probably, from the Rebel ranks than from McDowell's army, for thus far the battle has gone against them. You can see them scattered over the fields, beyond Mr. Lewis's.

The fight goes on. The artillery crashes louder than before. There is a continuous rattle of musketry. It is like the roaring of a hail-storm. Sherman and Keyes move down to the foot of the hill, near Mr. Lewis's. Burnside and Porter march across the turnpike. Franklin and Howard and Wilcox, who have been pushing south, turn towards the southeast. There are desperate hand-to-hand encounters. Cannon are taken and retaken. Gunners on both sides are shot while loading their pieces. Hundreds fall, and other hundreds leave the ranks. The woods toward Sudley Springs are filled with wounded men and fugitives, weak, thirsty, hungry, exhausted, worn down by the long morning march, want of sleep, lack of food, and the excitement of the hour.

Across the plains, towards Manassas, are other crowds,—disappointed, faint-hearted, defeated soldiers, fleeing for safety.

"We are defeated!"

"Our regiments are cut to pieces!"

"General Bartow is wounded and General Bee is killed!"

Thus they cry, as they hasten towards Manassas.[3] Officers and men in the Rebel ranks feel that the battle is all but lost. Union officers and men feel that it is almost won.

The Rebel right wing, far out upon the turnpike, has been folded back upon the centre; the centre has been driven in upon the left wing, and the left wing has been pushed back beyond Mr. Lewis's house. Griffin's and Rickett's batteries, which had been firing from the ridge west of the toll-gate, were ordered forward to the knoll from which the Rebel batteries had been driven.

"It is too far in advance," said General Griffin.

"The Fire Zouaves will support you," said General Barry.

"It is better to have them go in advance till we come into position; then they can fall back," Griffin replied.

"No; you are to move first, those are the orders. The Zouaves are already to follow on the double-quick."

"I will go; but, mark my words, they will not support me."

The battery galloped over the fields, descended the hill, crossed the ravine, advancing to the brow of the hill near Mrs. Henry's, followed by Rickett's battery, the Fire Zouaves, and the Fourteenth New York. In front of them, about forty or fifty rods distant, were the Rebel bat-

---

3: Rebel reports in *Rebellion Record*.

teries, supported by infantry. Griffin and Ricketts came into position, and opened a fire so terrible and destructive that the Rebel batteries and infantry were driven beyond the crest of the hill.

The field was almost won. Read what General Johnston says: "The long contest against fivefold odds, and heavy losses, especially of field officers, had greatly discouraged the troops of General Bee and Colonel Evans. The aspect of affairs was critical."

The correspondent of the Charleston Mercury writes: "When I entered on the field at two o'clock, the fortunes of the day were dark. The remnants of the regiments, so badly injured or wounded and worn, as they staggered out gave gloomy pictures of the scene. We could not be routed, perhaps, but it is doubtful whether we were destined to a victory."

The correspondent of the Richmond Despatch writes: "Fighting for hours under a hot sun, without a drop of water near, the conduct of our men could not be excelled; but human endurance has its bounds, *and all seemed about to be lost.*"

The battle surges around the house of Mrs. Henry. She is lying there amidst its thunders. Rebel sharpshooters take possession of it, and pick off Rickett's gunners. He turns his guns upon the house. Crash! crash! crash! It is riddled with grape and canister. Sides, roof, doors, and windows are pierced, broken, and splintered. The bed-clothes are cut into rags, and the aged woman instantly killed. The Rebel regiments melt away. The stream of fugitives toward Manassas grows more dense. Johnston has had more men and more guns engaged than McDowell; but he has been steadily driven. But Rebel reinforcements arrive from an unexpected quarter,—General Smith's brigade, from the Shenandoah. It comes into action in front of Wilcox. There are from two to three thousand men. General Smith is wounded almost at the first fire, and Colonel Elzey takes command. General Bonham sends two regiments, the Second and Eighth South Carolina. They keep south of Mrs. Henry's, and march on till they are in position to fire almost upon the backs of Griffin's and Rickett's gunners. They march through a piece of woods, reach the top of the hill, and come into line. Captain Imboden, of the Rebel battery, who is replying to Griffin, sees them. Who are they? He thinks they are Yankees flanking him. He wheels his guns, and is ready to cut them down with grape and canister. Captain Griffin sees them, and wheels his guns. Another instant, and he will sweep them away. He believes them to be Rebels. His gunners load with grape and canister.

"Do not fire upon them; they are your supports!" shouts Major Barry, riding up.

"No, sir; they are Rebels."

"They are your supports, just ordered up."

"As sure as the world, they are Rebels."

"You are mistaken, Captain; they are your supports."

The cannoneers stand ready to pull the lanyards, which will send a tornado through those ranks.

"Don't fire!" shouts the Captain.

The guns are wheeled again towards Mrs. Henry's, and the supposed supports are saved from destruction at the hand of Captain Griffin.

Captain Imboden, before ordering his men to fire upon the supposed Yankees, gallops nearer to them, to see who they are. He sees them raise their guns. There is a flash, a rattle and roll. Griffin's and Rickett's men and their horses go down in an instant! They rush on with a yell. There is sharp, hot, decisive work. Close musket-shots and sabre-strokes. Men are trampled beneath the struggling horses.

There are shouts and hurrahs. The few soldiers remaining to support Griffin and Rickett fire at the advancing Rebel brigade, but the contest is unequal; they are not able to hold in check the three thousand fresh troops. They fall back. The guns are in the hands of the Rebels. The day is lost. At the very moment of victory the line is broken. In an instant all is changed. A moment ago we were pressing on, but now we are falling back. Quick almost as the lightning's flash is the turning of the tide. All through a mistake! So great events sometimes hang on little things.

The unexpected volley, the sudden onset, the vigorous charge, the falling back, produces confusion in the Union ranks. Officers and men, generals and soldiers alike, are confounded. By a common impulse they begin to fall back across the turnpike. Unaccountably to themselves, and to the Rebel fugitives streaming towards Manassas, they lose strength and heart. The falling back becomes a retreat, a sudden panic and a rout. Regiments break and mix with others. Soldiers drop their guns and cartridge-boxes, and rush towards the rear.

I had watched the tide of battle through the day. Everything was favourable. The heat was intense, and I was thirsty. A soldier came past with a back-load of canteens freshly filled.

"Where did you find the water?"

"Over there in the woods, in the rear of Schenck's brigade."

I passed the brigade. Ayers's and Carlisle's batteries were there. I found the spring beyond a little hillock. While drinking, there was

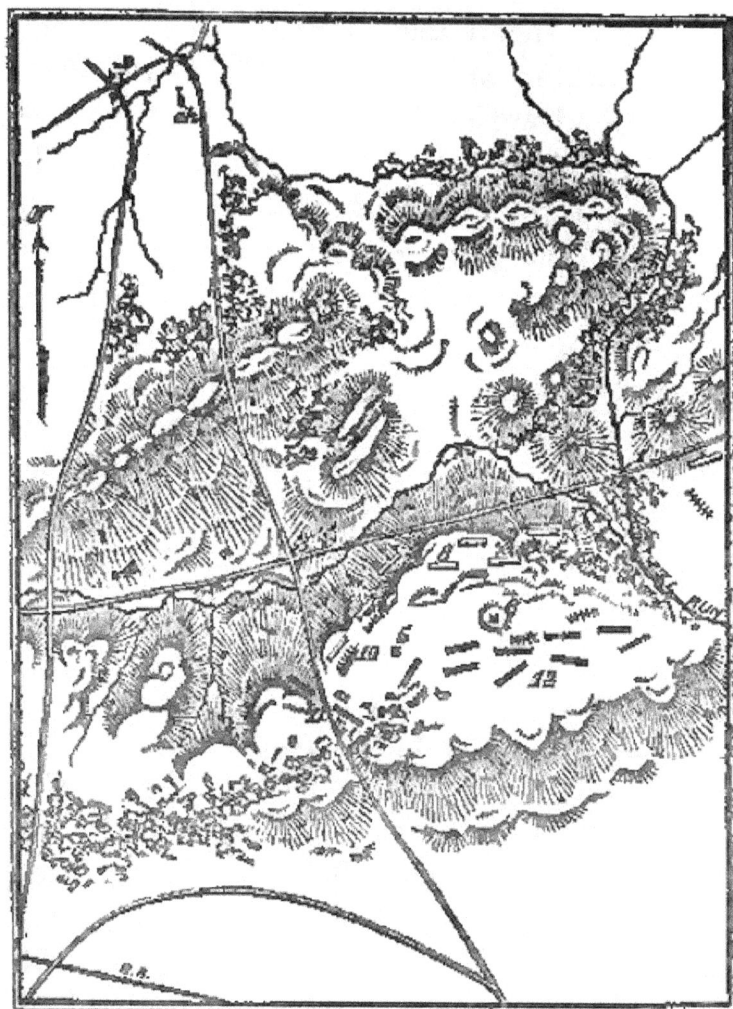

BULL RUN BATTLE-GROUND, July 21, 1861.

1  Stone Bridge.
2  Sudley Springs.
3  Toll-gate kept by Mr. Mathey
4  Mr. Dogan's house.
5  Mrs. Henry's.
6  Mr. Lewis's.
7  Wilcox's, Howard's, and Franklin's
   brigades.

8  Porter's and Burnside's brigades.
9  Sherman's and Keyes's brigades.
10 Griffin's and Rickett's batteries.
11 Rebel reinforcements which fired upon
   Griffin.
12 Position of Rebel army when the
   Union line gave way.
13 Ridge where the battle began.

sudden confusion in Schenck's brigade. There was loud talking, cannon and musketry firing, and a sudden trampling of horses. A squadron of Rebel cavalry swept past within a few rods of the spring, charging upon Schenck's brigade. The panic tide had come rolling to the rear. Ayers lashed his horses to a gallop, to reach Cub Run bridge. He succeeded in crossing it. He came into position to open upon the Rebels and to check their pursuit. The road was blocked with wagons. Frightened teamsters cut their horses loose and rode away. Soldiers, officers, and civilians fled towards Centreville, frightened at they knew not what. Blenker's brigade was thrown forward from Centreville to the bridge, and the rout was stopped. The Rebels were too much exhausted, too much amazed at the sudden and unaccountable breaking and fleeing of McDowell's army, to improve the advantage. They followed to Cub Run bridge, but a few cannon and musket shots sent them back to the Stone Bridge.

But at Blackburn's Ford General Jones crossed the stream to attack the retreating troops. General Davies, with four regiments and Hunt's battery, occupied the crest of a hill looking down towards the ford.

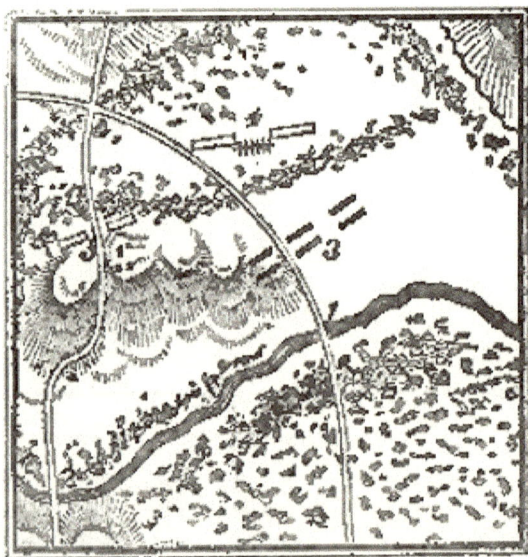

FIGHT AT BLACKBURN'S FORD, July 21, 1861.

1 Blackburn's Ford.                    4 Davies's brigade and batteries.
2 Mitchell's Ford.                     5 Richardson's brigade.
3 Rebel troops.

The Rebels marched through the woods upon the bank of the stream, wound along the hillside, filed through a farm-yard and halted in a hollow within a quarter of a mile of General Davies's guns.

"Lie down," said the General, and the four regiments dropped upon the ground. The six cannon and the gunners alone were in sight.

"Wait till they come over the crest of the hill; wait till I give the word," said the General to Captain Hunt.

The men stand motionless by their pieces. The long column of Rebels moves on. There is an officer on his horse giving directions. The long dark line throws its lengthening shadows upward in the declining sunlight, toward the silent cannon.

"Now let them have it!" The guns are silent no longer. Six flashes of light, and six sulphurous clouds are belched towards the moving mass. Grape and canister sweep them down. The officer tumbles from his horse, and the horse staggers to the earth. There are sudden gaps in the ranks. They stop advancing. Officers run here and there. Another merciless storm,—another,—another. Eighteen flashes a minute from those six pieces! Like grass before the mower the Rebel line is cut down. The men flee to the woods, utterly routed.

The attempt to cut off the retreat signally failed. It was the last attempt of the Rebels to follow up their mysterious victory. The rear-guard remained in Centreville till morning recovering five cannon which had been abandoned at Cub Run, which the Rebels had not secured, and then retired to Arlington.

So the battle was won and lost. So the hopes of the Union soldiers changed to sudden, unaccountable fear, and so the fear of the Rebels became unbounded exultation.

The sun had gone down behind the Blue Mountains, and the battle-clouds hung thick and heavy along the winding stream where the conflict had raged. It was a sad night to us who had gone out with such high hopes, who had seen the victory so nearly won and so suddenly lost. Many of our wounded were lying where they had fallen. It was a terrible night to them. Their enemies, some of them, were hard-hearted and cruel. They fired into the hospitals upon helpless men. They refused them water to quench their burning thirst. They taunted them in their hour of triumph, and heaped upon them bitterest curses. They were wild with the delirium of success, and treated their prisoners with savage barbarity. Any one who showed kindness to the prisoners or wounded was looked upon with suspicion. Says an English officer in the Rebel service:[4]

---

4: Estvan.

I made it my duty to seek out and attend upon the wounded, and the more so when I found that the work of alleviating their sufferings was performed with evident reluctance and want of zeal by many of those whose duty it was to do it. I looked upon the poor fellows only as suffering fellow-mortals, brothers in need of help, and made no distinction between friend and foe; nay, I must own that I was prompted to give the preference to the latter, for the reason that some of our men met with attention from their relations and friends, who had flocked to the field in numbers to see them. But in doing so I had to encounter opposition, and was even pointed at by some with muttered curses as a traitor to the cause of the Confederacy for bestowing any attention on the d—Yankees.

Notwithstanding the inhuman treatment they received at the hands of their captors, there were men on that field who never quailed,—men with patriotism so fervent, deep, and unquenchable, that they lay down cheerfully to their death-sleep. This officer in the Rebel service went out upon the field where the fight had been thickest. It was night. Around him were the dying and the dead. There was a young Union officer, with both feet crushed by a cannon-shot. There were tears upon his cheeks.

"Courage, comrade!" said the officer, bending over him; "the day will come when you will remember this battle as one of the things of the past."

"Do not give me false hopes, sir. It is all up with me. I do not grieve that I must die, for with these stumps I shall not live long."

He pointed to his mangled feet, and added: *"I weep for my poor, distracted country. Had I a second life to live, I would willingly sacrifice it for the cause of the Union!"*

His eyes closed. A smile lighted his countenance, as if, while on the border of another world, he saw once more those who were dearest on earth or in heaven. He raised himself convulsively, and cried, "Mother! Father!"

He was dead.

He sleeps upon the spot where he fell. His name is unknown, but his devotion to his country shall shine forevermore like a star in heaven!

When the Union line gave way, some of the soldiers were so stupefied by the sudden change that they were unable to move, and were taken prisoners. Among them was a Zouave, in red trousers. He was a tall, noble fellow. Although a prisoner, he walked erect, unabashed by his captivity. A Virginian taunted him, and called him by hard names.

"Sir," said the Zouave, "I have heard that yours was a nation of gentlemen, but your insult comes from a coward and a knave. I am your prisoner, but you have no right to fling your curses at me because I am unfortunate. Of the two, I consider myself the gentleman."[5]

The Virginian hung his head in silence, while other Rebel soldiers assured the brave fellow that he should not again be insulted. So bravery, true courage, and manliness will win respect even from enemies.

No accurate reports have been made of the number of men killed and wounded in this battle; but each side lost probably from fifteen hundred to two thousand men.

It was a battle which will always have a memorable place in the history of this Rebellion, because having won a victory, the slaveholders believed that they could conquer the North. They became more proud and insolent. They manifested their terrible hate by their inhuman treatment of the prisoners captured. They gave the dead indecent burial. The Rebel soldiers dug up the bones of the dead Union men, and carved them into ornaments, which they sent home to their wives and sweethearts. One girl wrote to her lover to "be sure and bring her Old Lincoln's *Skelp* " (scalp), so that the women as well as the men became fierce in their hatred. I have seen the letter, which was found upon a prisoner.

The North, although defeated, was not discouraged. There was no thought of giving up the contest, but, as you remember, there was a great uprising of the people, who determined that the war should go on till the Rebellion was crushed.

---

5: *Charleston Mercury.*

CHAPTER 4

# The Capture of Fort Henry

Tennessee joined the Southern Confederacy, but Kentucky resisted all the coaxing, threatening, and planning of the leaders of the Rebellion. Some Kentuckians talked of remaining neutral, of taking no part in the great contest; but that was not possible. The Rebels invaded the State, by sailing up the Mississippi and taking possession of Columbus,—a town twenty miles below the mouth of the Ohio. They also advanced from Nashville to Bowling Green. Then the State decided for the Union,—to stand by the old flag till the Rebellion should be crushed.

The Rebels erected two forts on the northern line of Tennessee. Looking at your map, you see that the Cumberland and Tennessee Rivers are near together where they enter the State of Kentucky. They are not more than twelve miles apart. The fort on the Tennessee River was named Fort Henry, the one on the Cumberland, Fort Donelson. A good road was cut through the woods between them, so that troops and supplies could be readily removed from one to the other. Fort Henry was on the eastern bank of the Tennessee, and Fort Donelson on the western bank of the Cumberland. They were very important places to the Rebels, for at high water in the winter the rivers are navigable for the largest steamboats,—the Cumberland to Nashville and the Tennessee to Florence, in Northern Alabama,—and it would be very easy to transport an army from the Ohio River to the very heart of the Southern Confederacy. The forts were built to prevent any such movement of the Union troops.

The bluffs of the Mississippi River at Columbus are two hundred feet high. There the Rebels erected strong batteries, planting heavy guns, with which they could sweep the Mississippi far up stream, and pour plunging shots with unobstructed aim upon any descending gun-

Thk Forts.

boat. They called it a Gibraltar, because of its strength. They said it
could not be taken, and that the Mississippi was closed to navigation till
the independence of the Southern Confederacy was acknowledged.

Early in the war it was seen that a fleet of gunboats would be
needed on the Western rivers, and Captain Andrew H. Foote of the
navy was placed in charge of their construction. They were built at
Cincinnati and St. Louis, and taken to Cairo, where they received their
armament, crews, and outfit.

You have heard of Cairo. I do not mean the ancient city on the
banks of the Nile, but the modern town on the tongue of land at the
mouth of the Ohio. Charles Dickens has given a description of the
place in one of his delightful books,—*Martin Chuzzlewit*. It was a forest, with a few log-huts, when Mark Tapley resided there, and all the
people were smitten with fever and ague. It is a town now, with several
thousand inhabitants. In the spring the town is sometimes overflowed,
and the people navigate the streets with boats and rafts. Pigs look out
of the chamber windows, and dogs, cats, and chickens live on the roofs
of houses at such times.

Let us take a look at the place as it appeared the first day of February, 1862. Stand with me on the levee, and look up the broad Ohio,—
the *la belle rivière*, as the French called it. There are from fifty to a hundred steamboats lying along the bank, with volumes of black smoke
rolling up from their tall chimneys, and puffs of steam vanishing in

47

the air. Among them are the gunboats,—a cross between a floating fort, a dredging-machine, and a mud-scow. The sailors, who have been tossed upon the ocean in stately ships, call them mud-*turkles*. There are thousands of soldiers on the steamboats and on the shore, waiting for the sailing of the expedition which is to make an opening in the line of Rebel defences. There are thousands of people busy as bees, loading and unloading the steamboats, rolling barrels and boxes.

When Mark Tapley and Martin Chuzzlewit were here it was muddy, and it is muddy now. There is fine, thin, sticky, slimy, splashy, thick, heavy, dirty mud. Thousands of men and thousands of mules and horses are treading it to mortar. It is mixed with slops from the houses and straw from the stables. You are reminded of the Slough of Despond described by Bunyan in the *Pilgrim's Progress*,—a place for all the filth, sin, and slime of this world. Christian was mired there, and Pliable nearly lost his life. If Bunyan had seen Cairo, he might have made the picture still more graphic. There are old houses, shanties, sheds, stables, pig-sties, wood-piles, carts, wagons, barrels, boxes, and all the old things you can imagine. Pigs live in the streets, and there are irrepressible conflicts between them and the hundreds of dogs. Water-carts, drays, army-wagons, and artillery go hub deep in the mud. Horses tug and strive, rear, kick, and flounder. Teamsters lose their footing. Soldiers wade leg deep in the street. There are sidewalks, but they are slippery, dangerous, and deceptive.

It is Sunday. A sweet day of rest in peaceful times, but in war there is not much observance of the Sabbath. It is midwinter, but a south-wind sweeps up the Mississippi, so mild and balmy that the blue-birds and robins are out. The steamboats are crowded with troops, who are waiting for orders to sail, they know not where. Groups stand upon the topmost deck. Some lie at full length in the warm sunshine. The bands are playing, the drums beating. Tug-boats are dancing, wheezing, and puffing in the stream, flitting from gunboat to gunboat.

The shops are open, and the soldiers are purchasing knickknacks,— tobacco, pipes, paper, and pens, to send letters to loved ones far away. At a gingerbread stall, a half-dozen are taking a lunch. The oyster-saloons are crowded. Boys are crying their newspapers. There are laughable and solemn scenes. Yonder is the hospital. A file of soldiers stand waiting in the street. A coffin is brought out. The fife begins its mournful air, the drum its muffled beat. The procession moves away, bearing the dead soldier to his silent home.

A few months ago he was a citizen, cultivating his farm upon the prairies, ploughing, sowing, reaping. But now the great reaper, Death, has gathered him in. He had no thought of being a soldier; but he was a patriot, and when his country called him he sprang to her aid. He yielded to disease, but not to the enemy. He was far from home and friends, with none but strangers to minister to his wants, to comfort him, to tell him of a better world than this. He gave his life to his country.

Although there is the busy note of preparation for the sailing of the fleet, there are some who remember that it is Sunday, and who find time to worship. The church-bells toll the hour. You tuck your pants into your boots, and pick your way along the slippery, slimy streets. There are a few ladies who brave the mud, wearing boots suited to the walking. Boots which have not been blacked for a fortnight are just as shiny as those cleaned but an hour ago. At the door of the church you do as everybody else does,—take a chip and scrape off the mud.

Half of the congregation are from the army and navy. Commodore Foote is there, a devout worshipper. Before coming to church he visited each gunboat of his fleet, called the crews together, read to them his general orders, that no unnecessary work should be done on the Sabbath, and enjoining upon the commanders the duty of having worship, and of maintaining a high moral character before the men.

Let us on Monday accept the kind invitation of Commodore Foote, and go on board the *Benton*, his flag-ship, and make an inspection of the strange-looking craft. It is unlike anything you ever saw at Boston or New York. It is like a great box on a raft. The sides are inclined, made of stout oak timbers and plated with iron. You enter through a porthole, where you may lay your hand upon the iron lips of a great gun, which throws a ball nine inches in diameter. There are fourteen guns, with stout oaken carriages. The men are moving about, exercising the guns,—going through the motions of loading and firing. How clean the floor! It is as white as soap and sand can make it. You must not spit tobacco-juice here, if you do, the courteous officer will say you are violating the rules. In the centre of the boat, down beneath the gun-deck in the hull, are the engines and the boilers, partly protected from any shot which may happen to come in at a porthole, or which may tear through the sides,—through the iron and the oak. Near the centre is the wheel. The top of the box, or the *casemate*, as it is called, is of oak timbers, and forms the upper deck. The pilot-house is on this upper deck, forward of the centre. In shape it is like a tunnel turned down. It is plated with thick iron.

There, in the hour of battle, the pilot will be, peeping out through narrow holes, his hands grasping the wheel and steering the vessel.

Its guns, which the sailors call its battery, are very powerful. There are two nine-inch guns, and also two sixty-four-pounders, rifled, at the bow. There are two forty-two-pounders at the stern, and those upon the side are thirty-twos and twenty-fours. There are rooms for the officers, but the men sleep in hammocks. They take their meals sitting on the gun-carriages, or cross-legged, like Turks, on the floor.

Captain Foote is the Commodore of the fleet. He points out to you the *Sacred Place* of the ship,—a secluded corner, where any one of the crew who loves to read his Bible and hold secret devotion may do so, and not be disturbed. He has given a library of good books to the crew, and he has persuaded them that it will be better for them to give up their allowance of grog than to drink it. He walks among the men, and has a kind word for all, and they look upon him as their father. They have confidence in him. How lustily they cheer him! Will they not fight bravely under such a commander?

********

On Monday afternoon, February 2nd, the gunboats *Cincinnati, Essex, St. Louis, Carondelet, Lexington, Tyler,* and *Conestoga* sailed from Cairo, accompanied by several river steamboats with ten regiments of troops. They went up the Ohio to Paducah, and entered the Tennessee River at dark. The next morning, about daylight, they anchored a few miles below Fort Henry. Commodore Foote made the *Cincinnati* his flag-ship.

A party of scouts went on shore and called at a farm-house. "You never will take Fort Henry," said the woman living there.

"O yes, we shall; we have a fleet of iron-clad gunboats," said one of the scouts.

"Your gunboats will be blown sky-high before they get up to the fort."

"Ah! how so?"

The woman saw that she was letting out a secret, and became silent. The scouts mistrusted that she knew something which might be desirable for them to know, and informed her that, unless she told all she knew, she must go with them a prisoner. She was frightened, and informed them that the river was full of torpedoes, which would blow up the gunboats.

The scouts reported to Commodore Foote. The river was searched with grappling-irons, and six infernal machines were fished up; but they were imperfectly constructed, and not one of them would explode.

Looking up the river from the deck of one of Commodore Foote's gunboats you see Panther Island, which is a mile from the fort. It is a long, narrow sand-bank, covered with a thicket of willows. There is the fort on the eastern bank. You see an irregular pile of earth, about fifteen feet above the river, with sand-bag embrasures, which at first sight you think are blocks of stone, but they are grain-sacks filled with sand. You count the guns, seventeen in all. One ten-inch columbiad, one sixty-pounder, twelve thirty-two-pounders, one twenty-four-pounder, and two twelve-pounders. They are nearly all pivoted, so that they may be pointed down the river against the boats or inland upon the troops. The river is nearly a half-mile wide, and on the opposite bank is another fort, not yet completed. All around Fort Henry you see rifle-pits and breastworks, enclosing twenty or thirty acres. Above and below the fort are creeks. The tall trees are cut down to obstruct the way, or to form an *abatis*, as it is called. It will not be an easy matter to take the fort from the land side. Inside these entrenchments is the Rebel camp,—log-huts and tents, with accommodations for several thousand men.

Commodore Foote has planned how to take the fort. He is confident that he can shell the Rebels out just as you can pound rats from a barrel or a box, and if General Grant will get in rear and watch his opportunity, they will all be caught.

General Grant lands two brigades of troops on the west side of the river, and three brigades on the east side, about four miles below the fort. Those on the west side are to look after any Rebels which may be in or around the unfinished fort, while those upon the east side, under General McClernand, work their way through the woods to gain the rear of the fort. This is the order to General McClernand:

> It will be the special duty of this command to prevent all reinforcements of Fort Henry or escape from it. Also to be held in readiness to charge and take Fort Henry by storm, promptly on receipt of orders.

General Grant and Commodore Foote agreed that the gunboats should commence the attack at twelve o'clock.

"I shall take the fort in about an hour," said the Commodore. "I shall commence firing when I reach the head of Panther Island, and it will take me about an hour to reach the fort, for I shall steam up slowly. I am afraid, General, that the roads are so bad the troops will not get round in season to capture the enemy. I shall take the fort before you get into position."

General Grant thought otherwise; but the roads were very muddy, and when the engagement commenced the troops were far from where they ought to have been.

Commodore Foote had prepared his instructions to the officers and crews of the gunboats several days before. They were brief and plain.

"The four iron-clad boats—the *Essex, Carondelet, St. Louis,* and *Cincinnati*—will keep in line. The *Conestoga, Lexington,* and *Tyler* will follow the iron-clads, and throw shells over those in advance."

To the commanders he said:

*"Do just as I do!"*

Addressing the crews, he said:

"Fire slowly, and with deliberate aim. There are three reasons why you should not fire rapidly. With rapid firing there is always a waste of ammunition. Your range is imperfect, and your shots go wide of the mark, and that encourages the enemy; and it is desirable not to heat the guns. If you fire slowly and deliberately, you will keep cool yourselves, and make every shot tell."

With such instructions, with all things ready,—decks cleared for action, guns run out, shot and shell brought up from the magazines and piled on deck,—confident of success, and determined to take the fort or go to the bottom, he waited the appointed hour.

The gunboats steam up slowly against the current, that the troops may have time to get into position in rear of the Rebel entrenchments. They take the channel on the west side of the island. The *Essex* is on the right of the battle line, nearest the island. Her Commander is William D. Porter, who comes from good stock. It was his father who commanded the *Essex* in the war with Great Britain in 1813, and who fought most gallantly a superior force,—two British ships, the *Phebe* and *Cherub,*—in the harbour of Valparaiso.

Next the *Essex* is the *Carondelet,* then the *Cincinnati,*—the flagship, with the brave Commodore on board,—and nearest the western shore the *St. Louis.* These are all iron-plated at the bows. Astern is the *Lexington,* the *Conestoga,* and the *Tyler.*

The boats reach the head of the island, and the fort is in full view. It is thirty-four minutes past twelve o'clock. There is a flash, and a great creamy cloud of smoke at the bow of the *Cincinnati.* An eight-inch shell screams through the air. The gunners watch its course. Their practised eyes follow its almost viewless flight. Your watch ticks fifteen seconds before you hear from it. You see a puff of smoke, a cloud of sand thrown up in the fort, and then hear the explosion. The com-

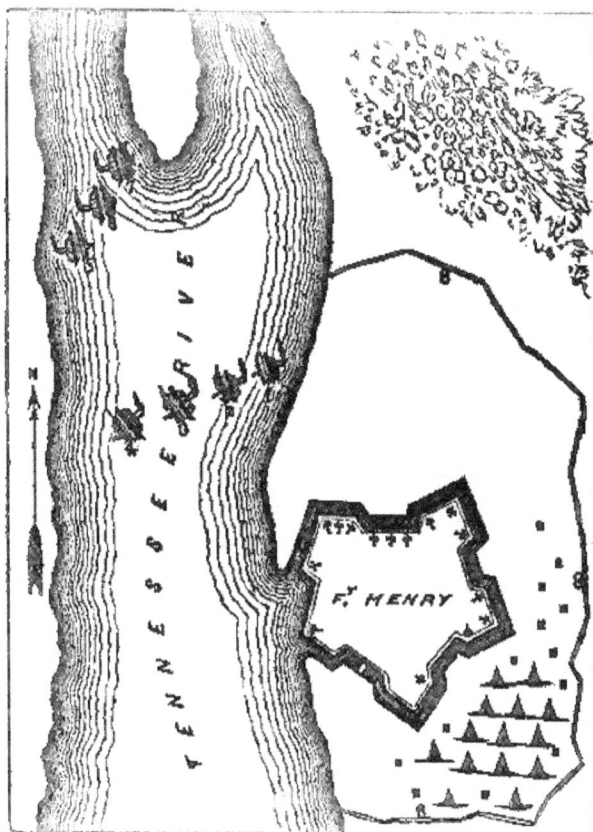

**FORT HENRY.**

manders of the other boats remember the instructions,— "Do just as I do!"—and from each vessel a shell is thrown. All fall within the fort, or in the encampment beyond, which is in sight. You can see the tents, the log-huts, the tall flagstaff. The fort accepts the challenge, and instantly the twelve guns which are in position to sweep the river open upon the advancing boats. The shot and shell plough furrows in the stream, and throw columns of water high in air.

Another round from the fleet. Another from the fort. The air is calm, and the thunder of the cannonade rolls along the valley, reverberating from hill to hill. Louder and deeper and heavier is the booming, till it becomes almost an unbroken peal.

There is a commotion in the Rebel encampment. Men run to and fro. They curl down behind the stumps and the fallen trees, to avoid the shot. Their huts are blown to pieces by the shells. You see the logs tossed like straws into the air. Their tents are torn into paper-rags. The hissing shells sink deep into the earth, and then there are sudden upheavals of sand, with smoke and flames, as if volcanoes were bursting forth. The parapet is cut through. Sand-bags are knocked about. The air is full of strange, hideous, mysterious, terrifying noises.

There are seven or eight thousand Rebel soldiers in the rifle-pits and behind the breastworks of the encampment in line of battle. They are terror-stricken. Officers and men alike lose all self-control. They run to escape the fearful storm. They leave arms, ammunition, tents, blankets, trunks, clothes, books, letters, papers, pictures,—everything. They pour out of the entrenchments into the road leading to Dover, a motley rabble. A small steamboat lies in the creek above the fort. Some rush on board and steam up river with the utmost speed. Others, in their haste and fear, plunge into the creek and sink to rise no more. All fly except a brave little band in the fort.

The gunboats move straight on, slowly and steadily. Their fire is regular and deliberate. Every shot goes into the fort. The gunners are blinded and smothered by clouds of sand. The gun-carriages are crushed, splintered, and overturned. Men are cut to pieces. Something unseen tears them like a thunderbolt. The fort is full of explosions. The heavy rifled gun bursts, crushing and killing those who serve it. The flagstaff is splintered and torn, as by intensest lightning.

Yet the fort replies. The gunners have the range of the boats, and nearly every shot strikes the iron plating. They are like the strokes of sledge-hammers, indenting the sheets, starting the fastenings, breaking the tough bolts. The *Cincinnati* receives thirty-one shots, the *Essex* fifteen, the *St. Louis* seven, and the *Carondelet* six.

Though struck so often, they move on. The distance lessens. Another gun is knocked from its carriage in the fort,—another,—another. There are signs that the contest is about over, that the Rebels are ready to surrender. But a shot strikes the *Essex* between the iron plates. It tears through the oaken timbers and into one of the steam-boilers. There is a great puff of steam. It pours from the portholes, and the boat is enveloped in a cloud. She drops out of the line of battle. Her engines stop and she floats with the stream. Twenty-eight of her crew are scalded, among them her brave commander.

The Rebels take courage. They spring to their guns, and fire rapidly and wildly, hoping and expecting to disable the rest of the fleet. But the Commodore does not falter; he keeps straight on as if nothing had happened. An eighty-pound shell from the *Cincinnati* dismounts a gun, killing or wounding every gunner. The boats are so near that every shot is sure to do its work. The fire of the boats increases while the fire of the fort diminishes. Coolness, determination, energy, perseverance, and power win the day. The Rebel flag comes down, and the white flag goes up. They surrender. Cheers ring through the fleet. A boat puts out from the *St. Louis.* An officer jumps ashore, climbs the torn embankment, stands upon the parapet and waves the Stars and Stripes. "Hurrah! hurrah! hurrah!" You hear it echoing from shore to shore.

General Lloyd Tilghman commanded in the fort. He went on board the flag-ship.

"What terms do you grant me?" he asked.

"Your surrender must be unconditional, sir. I can grant you no other terms."

"Well, sir, if I must surrender, it gives me pleasure to surrender to so brave an officer as you."

"You do perfectly right to surrender, sir; but I should not have done it on any condition."

"Why so? I do not understand you."

"Because I was fully determined to capture the fort or go to the bottom."

"I thought I had you, Commodore, but you were too much for me."

"How could you fight against the old flag, General?"

"Well, it did come hard at first; but if the North had only let us alone, there would have been no trouble. They would not abide by the Constitution."

"You are mistaken, General, and the whole South is mistaken. The North have always been willing that the South should have all her rights, under the Constitution. The South began the war, and she will be responsible for the blood which has been shed to-day."

Thus, in an hour and twelve minutes, the fort which the Rebels confidently expected would prevent the gunboats from ascending the river was forced to surrender, and there was unobstructed water communication to the very heart of the Southern Confederacy. Their line of defence was broken.

There was but little loss of life in this engagement,—twenty to thirty killed and wounded on each side. If the Rebel army had not fled almost at the first fire, there would have been terrible slaughter. When Commodore Foote was informed that there were several thousand troops in the fortifications, said he, "I am sorry for it, because if they stand their ground there will be great destruction of life from the heavy shells; for I shall take the fort or sink with the ships."

If the troops under General Grant had been in position to have intercepted the Rebel force, the whole panic-stricken crowd would have been captured, but being delayed by the mud, the fleet-footed Rebels were far on their way towards Fort Donelson when General Grant reached the rear of the entrenchments. In their haste and terror the Rebels abandoned nine pieces of field artillery on the road, and a large supply of ammunition.

The battle was fought on Thursday. On Friday Commodore Foote returned to Cairo, to send his despatches to Washington, also to repair his gunboats and to see that the poor scalded men on the *Essex* were well taken care of.

I was writing, at Cairo, the account of the battle. It was past midnight when the Commodore came to my room. He sat down, and told me what I have written of his plan of the battle, and his talk with General Tilghman. He could not sit still. He was weary and exhausted with his labours. "I am afraid, Commodore, that you have overworked. You must have rest and sleep," I remarked.

"Yes, I have been obliged to work pretty hard, and need rest, but I never slept better in my life than night before last, and I never prayed more fervently than on yesterday morning before going into the battle; but I couldn't sleep last night for thinking of those poor fellows on board the *Essex*," was the reply.

On Sunday morning he was at church as usual. The minister was late. The people thought there would be no meeting, and were about to leave the house. Commodore Foote went to one of the Elders of the church, and urged him to conduct the worship. The Elder declined. But the Commodore never let slip an opportunity for doing good. He was always ready to serve his country and his God. He went into the pulpit, read a chapter, offered a prayer, and preached a short sermon from the words,— *"Let not your hearts be troubled. Ye believe in God; believe also in me."* It was an exhortation for all men to believe on the Lord Jesus Christ as the Saviour of the world. Some who heard him, as they went home from church, said that they also believed in Commodore Foote!

To him belongs the credit not only of taking Fort Henry, but of planning the expedition. When the true history of this Rebellion is written, you will see how important a thing it was, how great its results, and you will admire more and more the sterling patriotism and unswerving Christian principles of a man who struck this first great blow, and did so much towards crushing the Rebellion.

CHAPTER 5

# The Capture of Fort Donelson

General Grant's plan for taking Fort Donelson was, to move the first and second divisions of his army across the country, and attack the fort in the rear, while another division, accompanied by the gunboats, should go up the Cumberland and attack the fort from that direction. Commodore Foote informed the General that it was necessary to repair the gunboats which had been injured before commencing operations; but General Grant determined to make no delay on that account. Without fully perfecting his arrangements, or calculating the time needed for the steamboats to go from Fort Henry down to the Ohio and up the Cumberland, he ordered the two divisions to march. General Lewis Wallace was left at Fort Henry with a brigade, while six regiments of his division, the third, were embarked on the steamboats, which sailed down the Tennessee in fine style, turning back other boats, and all proceeded up the Cumberland.

There are steep hills, sandy plains, deep ravines, trickling brooks, and grand old forest-trees between Fort Henry and Fort Donelson. The road winds along the hillsides, over the plains, and descends into the ravines. There are but few farm-houses, for the soil is unproductive and the forests remain almost as they have been for hundreds of years. The few farmers who reside there live mainly on hog and hominy. They cultivate a few acres of corn, but keep a great many pigs, which live in the woods and fatten upon acorns and hickory-nuts.

The regiments which marched to Fort Donelson bivouacked the first night beside a stream of water about four miles from Fort Henry. They had no tents. They had been in barracks at Cairo through December and January, but now they must lie upon the ground, wrapped in their blankets. The nights were cold, and the ground was frozen. They cut down the tall trees and kindled great fires, which roared and crackled in the frosty air. They scraped the dead leaves into heaps and made them beds. They saw the pigs in the woods. Crack! crack! went their rifles, and they had roast sparerib and pork-steaks,—delicious eating to hungry men. The forest was all aglow with the hundreds of fires. The men told stories, toasted their toes, looked into the glowing coals, thought perhaps of home, of the dear ones there, then wrapped their blankets about them and went to sleep. Out towards Fort Donelson the pickets stood at their posts and looked into the darkness, watching for the enemy through the long winter night. But no Rebels appeared. They had been badly frightened at Fort Henry. They had recovered from their terror, however, and had determined to make a brave stand at Fort Donelson. They had been reinforced by a large body of troops from General Albert Sidney Johnston's army at Bowling Green, in Kentucky, and from General Lee's army in Virginia.

General Grant's two divisions, which marched across the country, numbered about fifteen thousand. There were four brigades in the first division,—Colonel Oglesby's, Colonel W. H. L. Wallace's, Colonel McArthur's, and Colonel Morrison's. Colonel Oglesby had the Eighth, Eighteenth, Twenty-ninth, Thirtieth, and Thirty-first Illinois regiments. Colonel Wallace's was composed of the Eleventh, Twentieth, Forty-fifth, and Forty-eighth Illinois regiments. In Colonel McArthur's were the Second, Ninth, Twelfth, and Forty-first Illinois, and in Colonel Morrison's the Seventeenth and Forty-ninth Illinois regiments.

Schwartz's, Taylor's, Dresser's, and McAllister's batteries accompanied this division.

There were three brigades in the second division. The first, under the command of Colonel Cook, was composed of the Seventh Illinois, Twelfth Iowa, Thirteenth Missouri, and Fifty-second Indiana.

Colonel Lauman commanded the second brigade, composed of the Second, Seventh, Fourteenth, and Twenty-eighth Iowa regiments, the Fifty-second Indiana, and Colonel Birges's regiment of sharpshooters.

The third brigade, commanded by Colonel Morgan L. Smith, was composed of the Eighth Missouri and Eleventh Indiana.

Major Cavender's regiment of Missouri artillery was attached to this division, composed of three full batteries,—Captain Richardson's, Captain Stone's, and Captain Walker's.

The Fourth Illinois cavalry and three or four companies of cavalry were distributed among the brigades.

Colonel Birges's sharpshooters were picked men, who had killed many bears, deer, and wolves in the Western woods. They could take unerring aim, and bring down a squirrel from the top of the highest trees. They wore gray uniforms of felt, with close-fitting skull-caps, and buffalo-skin knapsacks, and a powder-horn. They were swift runners. Each man carried a whistle. They had signal-calls for advancing, or retreating, or moving to the right or the left. They glided through the forests like fleet-footed deer, or crept as stealthily as an Indian along the ravines and through the thickets. They were tough, hearty, daring, courageous men. They thought it no great hardship to march all day, and lie down beside a log at night without supper. They wanted no better fun than to creep through the underbrush and pick off the Rebels, whirling in an instant upon their backs after firing a shot, to reload their rifles. Although attached to Lauman's brigade, they were expected in battle to go where they could do the most service.

As you go up the Cumberland River, and approach the town of Dover, you see a high hill on the west bank. It is crowned with an embankment of earth, which runs all round the top with many angles. At the foot of the hill are two other embankments, fifteen or twenty feet above the water. There are seventeen heavy guns in these works. Two of them throw long bolts of iron, weighing one hundred and twenty-eight pounds, but most of the guns are thirty-two-pounders.

If you go into the batteries and into the fort, and run your eye along the guns, you will see that all of them can be aimed at a gunboat in the river. They all point straight down stream, and a concentrated fire can be poured upon a single boat. The river makes a bend as it approaches the batteries, so that the boats will be exposed on their bows and sides.

A mile above the fort you see the little village of Dover. Beyond the village a creek comes in. It is high water, and the creek is too deep to be forded.

On the south side of the hill, beyond the fort, between the fort and the village, are log-huts, where the Rebel troops have been encamped through the winter. A stream of clear running water comes down from the hills west of the village, where you may fill your canteen.

Going up the hill into the fort, and out to its northwest angle, you see that the fortifications which the Rebels have thrown up consist of three distinct parts,—the fort and the water-batteries, a line of breast-works west of the village, called field-works, and a line of rifle-pits outside of the field-works. You begin at the northwest angle of the fort, face to the southwest, and walk along the field-work which is on the top of a sharp ridge. The embankment is about four feet high. There are a great many angles, with embrasures for cannon. You look west from these embrasures, and see that the ground is much broken. There are hills and hollows, thick brush and tall trees. In some places the trees have been cut down to form an *abatis*, an obstruction, the limbs lopped off and interlocked.

As you walk on, you come to the Fort Henry and Dover road. Crossing that, instead of walking southwest, you make a gradual turn towards the southeast, and come to another road, which leads from Dover southwest towards Clarksville and Nashville. Crossing that, you come to the creek which empties into the Cumberland just above the town. The distance from the creek back to the fort, along the line of

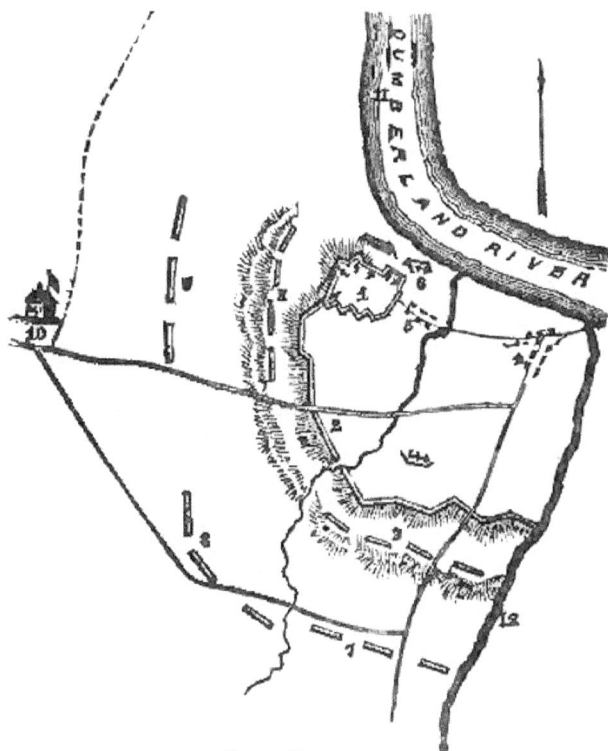

FORT DONELSON.

| | |
|---|---|
| 1 The Fort. | 7 General McClernand's division. |
| 2 Field-works. | 8 General Lewis Wallace's division. |
| 3 3 Rifle-pits. | 9 General Smith's division. |
| 4 Town of Dover. | 10 General Grant's Head-quarters. |
| 5 Log-huts. | 11 Gunboats. |
| 6 Water-batteries. | 12 Light Creek. |

breastworks, is nearly two miles. Going back once more to the north-west angle of the fort, you see that the slope of the hill is very steep outside the works. You go down the slope, planting your feet into the earth to keep from tumbling headlong. When you reach the bottom of the ravine you do not find a level piece of ground, but ascend another ridge. It is not as high as the ridge along which you have travelled to take a view of the works. The slope of this outer ridge runs down to a meadow. The Rebels have cut down the tall trees, and made a line of rifle-pits. The logs are piled one above another, as the backwoodsman builds a log-fence. There is a space five or six inches wide between the upper log and the one below it. They have dug a trench behind, and the dirt is thrown outside.

The Rebel riflemen can lie in the trench, and fire through the space between the logs upon the Union troops if they attempt to advance upon the works. You look down this outer slope. It is twenty rods to the bottom, and it is covered with fallen trees. You think it almost im-possible to climb over such a hedge and such obstructions. You see a cleared field at the base of the hill, and a farm-house beyond the field, on the Fort Henry road, which is General Grant's headquarters. The whole country is broken into hills, knolls, and ridges. It reminds you of the waves you have seen on the ocean or on the lakes in a storm.

General Floyd, who was Secretary of War under Buchanan, and who stole all the public property he could lay his hands on while in office, commanded the Rebel forces. He arrived on the 13th. General Pillow and Brigadier-General Johnson were placed in command of the troops on the Rebel left wing west of the town. General Buck-ner commanded those in the vicinity of the fort. General Floyd had the Third, Tenth, Eighteenth, Twenty-sixth, Thirtieth, Thirty-second, Forty-first, Forty-second, Forty-Eighth, Forty-ninth, Fiftieth, Fifty-first, and Fifty-third regiments of Tennessee troops, the Second and Eighth Kentucky, the First, Third, Fourth, Fourteenth, Twentieth, and Twenty-sixth Mississippi regiments, the Seventh Texas, Fifteenth and Twenty-seventh Alabama, the Thirty-sixth, Fiftieth, Fifty-first, and Fifty-sixth Virginia, also two battalions of Tennessee infantry, and a brigade of cavalry. He had Murray's, Porter's, Graves's, Maney's, Jack-son's, Guy's, Ross's, and Green's batteries, in all about twenty-three thousand men, with forty-eight pieces of field artillery, and seventeen heavy guns in the fort and water-batteries.

General Grant knew but little of the ground, or the fortifications, or of the Rebel forces, but he pushed boldly on.

On the morning of the 12th the troops left their bivouac, where they had enjoyed their roast spareribs and steaks, and marched towards the fort. The cavalry swept the country, riding through the side roads and foot-paths, reconnoitring the ground, and searching for Rebel pickets.

Soon after noon they came in sight of the Rebel encampments. The ground was thoroughly examined. No Rebels were found outside the works, but upon the hills within the entrenchments dark masses of men could be seen, some busily at work with axes and shovels. Regiments were taking positions for the expected attack; but it was already evening, and the advancing army rested for the night.

## THURSDAY

The night had been cold, but on the morning of the 13th there were breezes from the southwest, so mild and warm that the spring birds came. The soldiers thought that the winter was over. The sky was cloudless. All the signs promised a pleasant day. The troops were early awake,—replenishing the fading fires, and cooking breakfasts. With the dawn the sharpshooters and pickets began their work. There was a rattling musket-fire in the ravines.

Before the sun rose the Rebel batteries began throwing shells across the ravines and hills, aiming at the camp-fires of Colonel Oglesby's brigade. Instantly the camp was astir. The men fell into line with a hurrah, the cannoneers sprang to their guns, all waiting for the orders.

The clear, running brook which empties into the Cumberland between Dover and Fort Donelson winds through a wide valley. It divides the Rebel field-works into two parts,—those west of the town and those west of the fort. The road from Fort Henry to Dover crosses the valley in a southeast direction. As you go towards the town, you see at your left hand, on the hill, through the branches of the trees, the Rebel breastworks, and you are almost within musket-shot.

General McClernand moved his division down the Dover road, while General Smith remained opposite the northwest angle of the fort. Oglesby's brigade had the advance, followed by nearly all of the division. The batteries moved along the road, but the troops marched through the woods west of the road. The artillery came into position on the hills about a half-mile from the breastworks, and opened fire,—Taylor, Schwartz, and Dresser west of the town, and Cavender, with his heavy guns, west of the fort.

The Rebel batteries began a furious fire. Their shells were excellently aimed. One struck almost at the feet of Major Cavender as he was sighting a gun, but it did not disturb him. He took deliberate aim, and sent shell after shell whizzing into the fort. Another shot fell just in rear of his battery. A third burst overhead. Another struck one of Captain Richardson's men in the breast, whirling him into the air, killing him instantly.

Major Cavender moved his pieces, and then returned the fire with greater zeal. Through the forenoon the forests echoed the terrific cannonade, mingled with the sharp crack of the riflemen, close under the breastworks.

At noon the infantry fight began. West of the town, in addition to the line of rifle-pits and breastworks, the Rebels had thrown up a small redoubt, behind which their batteries were securely posted. General McClernand decided to attack it. He ordered Colonel Wallace to direct the assault. The Forty-eighth, Seventeenth, and Forty-ninth Illinois regiments were detached from the main force, and placed under the command of Colonel Hayne, of the Forty-eighth, for a storming party. McAllister's battery was wheeled into position to cover the attack.

They form in line at the base of the hill. The shells from the Rebel batteries crash among the trees. The Rebel riflemen keep up a rattling fire from the thickets. The troops are fresh from the prairies. This is their first battle, but at the word of command they advance across the intervening hollows and ascend the height, facing the sheets of flame which burst from the Rebel works. They fire as they advance. It is not a rush and a hurrah, but a steady movement. Men begin to drop from the line, but there is no wavering. They who never before heard the sounds of battle stand like veterans. The Rebel line in front of them extends farther than their own. The Forty-fifth Illinois goes to the support of Wallace. The Rebels throw forward reinforcements. There is a continuous roll of musketry, and quick discharges of cannon. The attacking force advances nearer and still nearer, close up to the works. Their gallantry does not fail them; their courage does not falter; but they find an impassable obstruction,—fallen trees, piles of brush, and rows of sharp stakes. Taylor's battery gallops up the road, and opens a rapid fire, but the Rebel sharpshooters pick off his gunners. It is madness to remain, and the force retires beyond the reach of the Rebel musketry; but they are not disheartened. They have hardly begun to fight.

Colonel Birges's sharpshooters are sent for. They move down through the bushes, and creep up in front of the Rebel lines. There are jets of flame and wreaths of blue smoke from their rifles. The Rebel pickets are driven back. The sharpshooters work their way still nearer to the trenches. The bushes blaze. There are mysterious puffs of smoke from the hollows, from stumps, and from the roots of trees. The Rebel gunners are compelled to let their guns remain silent, and the infantry dare not show their heads above the breastworks. They lie close. A Rebel soldier raises his slouched hat on his ramrod. Birges's men see it, just over the parapet. Whiz! The hat disappears. The Rebels chuckle that they have outwitted the Yankee.

"Why don't you come out of your old fort?" shouts a sharpshooter, lying close behind a tree.

"Why don't you come in?" is the answer from the breastworks.

"O, you are cowards!" says the voice at the stump.

"When are you going to take the fort?" is the response from the breastwork.

The cannonade lasted till night. Nothing had been gained, but much had been lost, by the Union army. There were scores of men lying in the thickets, where they had fallen. There were hundreds in the hospitals. The gunboats and the expected reinforcements had not arrived. The Rebels outnumbered General Grant's force by several thousand, but fortunately they did not know it. General Grant's provisions were almost gone. There was no meat, nothing but hard bread. The south-wind of the morning had changed to the east. It was mild then, but piercing now. The sky, so golden at the dawn, was dark and lowering, with clouds rolling up from the east. The rain began to fall. The roads were miry, the dead leaves slippery. The men had thrown aside their overcoats and blankets. They had no shelter, no protection. They were weary and exhausted with the contest. They were cold, wet, and hungry. The rain increased. The wind blew more furiously. It wailed through the forest. The rain changed to hail. The men lay down upon frozen beds, and were covered with icy sheets. It grew colder. The hail became snow. The wind increased to a gale, and whirled the snow into drifts. The soldiers curled down behind the stumps and fallen trees. They built great fires. They walked, ran, thumped their feet upon the frozen ground, beat their fingers till the blood seemed starting from beneath the nails. The thermometer sank almost to zero. It was a night of horror, not only outside, but inside the Rebel lines. The Southern soldiers were kept in the entrenchments, in the rifle-pits, and ditches, to be in readiness to repel an assault. They could not keep up great, roaring fires, for fear of inviting a night attack. Through the long hours the soldiers of both armies kept their positions, exposed to the fury of the winter storm, not only the severest storm of the season, but the wildest and coldest that had been known for many years in that section of the country.

## FRIDAY

Friday morning dawned, and with the first rays of light the rifles cracked in the frosty air. The sharpshooters, though they had passed a sleepless night, were in their places behind rocks and stumps and trees. Neither army was ready to recommence the struggle. General Grant was out of provisions. The transports, with supplies and reinforcements, had not arrived. Only one gunboat, the *Carondelet*, had come.

It was a critical hour. What if the Rebels, with their superior force, should march out from their entrenchments and make an attack? How long could the half-frozen, exhausted, hungry men maintain their ground? Where were the gunboats? Where the transports? Where the reinforcements? There were no dark columns of smoke rising above the forest-trees, indicating the approach of the belated fleet.

General Grant grew anxious. Orders were despatched to General Wallace at Fort Henry to hasten over with his troops. There was no thought of giving up the enterprise.

"We came here to take the fort, and we intend to do it," said Colonel Oglesby.

A courier came dashing through the woods. He had been on the watch three miles down the river, looking for the gunboats. He had descried a dense cloud of black smoke in the distance, and started with the welcome intelligence. They were coming. The *Carondelet*, which had been lying quietly in the stream below the fort, steamed up against the current, and tossed a shell towards the Rebels. The deep boom of the columbiad echoed over the hills of Tennessee. The troops answered with a cheer from the depths of the forest. They could see the trailing black banners of smoke from the steamer. They became light-hearted. The wounded lying in the hospitals, stiff, sore, mangled, their wounds undressed, chilled, frozen, covered with ice and snow, forgot their sufferings. So the fire of patriotism burned within their hearts, which could not be quenched by sufferings worse than death itself.

The provisions, troops, and artillery were landed at a farm, three miles below the fort. A road was cut through the woods, and communication opened with the army.

A division was organized under General Lewis Wallace. Colonel Cruft commanded the first brigade, composed of the Thirty-first and Forty-fourth Indiana, the Seventeenth and Twenty-fifth Kentucky regiments.

The second brigade was composed of the Forty-sixth, Fifty-seventh, and Fifty-eighth Illinois regiments. It had no brigade commander, and was united to the third brigade, commanded by Colonel Thayer. The third brigade was composed of the First Nebraska, the Sixteenth, Fifty-eighth, and Sixty-eighth Ohio regiments. Several other regiments arrived while the fight was going on, but they were held in reserve, and had but little if any part in the action.

Wallace's division was placed between General Smith's and General McClernand's, near General Grant's headquarters, on the road leading from Fort Henry to Dover. It took all day to get the troops into position and distribute food and ammunition, and there was no fighting except by the skirmishers and sharpshooters.

At three o'clock in the afternoon the gunboats steamed slowly up stream to attack the water-batteries. Commodore Foote repeated the instructions to the commanders and crews that he made before the attack at Fort Henry,—to fire slow, take deliberate aim, and keep cool.

The *Pittsburg, St. Louis, Louisville,* and *Carondelet,* iron-plated boats, had the advance, followed by the three wooden boats,—the *Tyler, Lexington,* and *Conestoga.* A bend in the river exposed the sides of the gunboats to a raking fire from the batteries, while Commodore Foote could only use the bow guns in reply. The fort on the hill was so high above the boats that the muzzles of the guns could not be elevated far enough to hit it. Commodore Foote directed the boats to engage the water-batteries, and pay no attention to the guns of the fort till the batteries were silenced; then he would steam past them and pour broadsides into the fort.

As soon as the gunboats rounded the point of land a mile and a half below the fort, the Rebels opened fire, and the boats replied. There was excellent gunnery. The shots from the fort and batteries fell upon the bows of the boats, or raked their sides; while the shells from the boats fell plump into the batteries, cutting the embankments, or sinking deep in the side of the hill and bursting with tremendous explosions, throwing the earth upon the gunners in the trenches. Steadily onward moved the boats, pouring all their shells into the lower works. It was a continuous storm,—an unbroken roll of thunder. There were constant explosions in the Rebel trenches. The air was filled with pieces of iron from the exploding shells and lumps of frozen earth thrown up by the solid shot. The Rebels fled in confusion from the four-gun battery, running up the hill to the entrenchments above.

The fight had lasted an hour, and the boats were within five hundred feet of the batteries; fifteen minutes more and the Commodore would be abreast of them, and would rake them from bottom to top with his tremendous broadsides. But he had reached the bend of the river; the eight-gun battery could cut him through crosswise, while the guns on the top of the hill could pour plunging shots upon his decks. The Rebels saw their advantage, and worked their guns with all their might. The boats were so near that every Rebel shot reached its mark. A solid shot cut the rudder-chains of the *Carondelet* and she became unmanageable. The thirty-two-pound balls went through the oak sides of the boats as you can throw peas through wet paper. Another shot splintered the helm of the *Pittsburg*, and that boat also became unmanageable. A third shot crashed through the pilot-house of the *St. Louis*, killing the pilot instantly. The Commodore stood by his side, and was sprinkled with the blood of the brave, unfortunate man. The shot broke the wheel and knocked down a timber which wounded the Commodore in the foot. He sprang to the deck, limped to another steering apparatus, and endeavoured with his own hands to keep the vessel head to the stream; but that apparatus also had been shot away. Sixty-one shots had struck the *St. Louis*; some had passed through from stem to stern. The *Louisville* had received thirty-five shots. Twenty-six had crashed into and through the *Carondelet*. One of her guns had burst, killing and wounding six of the crew. The *Pittsburg* had been struck twenty-one times. All but the *Louisville*, of the iron-plated boats, were unmanageable. At the very last moment— when the difficulties had been almost overcome—the Commodore was obliged to hoist the signal for retiring. Ten minutes more,—five hundred feet more,—and the Rebel trenches would have been swept from right to left, their entire length. When the boats began to drift down the stream they were running from the trenches, deserting their guns, to escape the fearful storm of grape and canister which they knew would soon sweep over them. Fifty-four were killed and wounded in this attack.

At night Commodore Foote sat in the cabin of the *St. Louis* and wrote a letter to a friend. His wound was painful, but he thought not of his own sufferings. He frequently asked how the wounded men were getting along, and directed the surgeons to do everything possible for their comfort. This is what he wrote to his friend:

> While I hope ever to rely on Him who controls all things, and to say from my heart, 'Not unto us, but unto thee, O Lord, belongs the glory,' yet I feel bad at the result of our attack on Fort Donelson. To see brave officers and men, who say they will go where I lead them, fall by my side, it makes me sad to lead them to almost certain death.

So passed Friday. The gunboats were disabled. No impression had been made on the fort. General Grant determined to place his army in position on the hills surrounding the fort, throw up entrenchments, and wait till the gunboats could be repaired. Then there would be a combined attack, by water and by land, which he hoped would reduce the place.

On Friday evening there was a council of war at General Floyd's headquarters in the town. General Buckner, General Johnson, General Pillow, Colonel Baldwin, Colonel Wharton, and other commanders of brigades were present. General Floyd said that he was satisfied that General Grant would not renew the attack till the gunboats were repaired, and till he had received reinforcements. He thought that the whole available force of Union troops would be hurried up by steamboat from St. Louis, Cincinnati, and Cairo; and that when they arrived a division would be marched up the river towards Clarksville, above Dover, and that they in the fort would be starved out and forced to surrender without a battle. It was very good and correct reasoning on the part of General Floyd, who did not care to be taken prisoner after he had stolen so much public property. It was just what General Grant intended to do. He knew that by such a course the fort would be obliged to surrender, and he would save the lives of his men.

General Floyd proposed to attack General Grant at daylight on Saturday morning, by throwing one half of the Rebel army, under Pillow and Johnson, upon McClernand's division. By making the attack then in overwhelming force, he felt pretty sure he could drive McClernand back upon General Wallace. General Buckner, with the other half of the army, was to push out from the northwest angle of the fort at the same time, attack General Wallace, and force him back upon General McClernand, which would throw the Union troops into confusion. By adopting this plan he hoped to win a victory, or if not that, he could open a way of escape to the whole army. The plan was agreed to by the other officers, and preparations were made for the attack. The soldiers received extra rations and a large quantity of ammunition. The caissons of the artillery were filled up, and the regiments placed in position to move early in the morning.

## SATURDAY

General B. R. Johnson led the Rebel column, and Colonel Baldwin's brigade the advance. It was composed of the First and Fourteenth Mississippi and the Twenty-sixth Tennessee regiments. The next brigade was Colonel Wharton's. It was composed of the Fiftieth and Fifty-first Virginia. McCousland's brigade was composed of the Thirty-sixth and Fifty-sixth Virginia; Davidson's brigade was composed of the Seventh Texas, Eighth Kentucky, and Third Mississippi; Colonel Drake's brigade was composed of the Fourth and Twentieth Mississippi, Garven's battalion of riflemen, Fifteenth Arkansas, and a Tennessee regiment. Hieman's brigade was composed of the Tenth, Thirtieth, and Forty-eighth Tennessee, and the Twenty-seventh Alabama. There were about thirty pieces of artillery, and twelve thousand men in this column.

McArthur's brigade of McClernand's division was on the extreme right, and a short distance in rear of Oglesby. The Rebels moved down the Union Ferry road, which leads southwest towards Clarksville, which brought them nearly south of Oglesby and McArthur. Oglesby's regiments stood, the Eighth Illinois on the right, then the Twenty-ninth, Thirtieth, and Thirty-first, counting towards the left. Schwartz's battery was on the right and Dresser's on the left. Wallace's brigade was formed with the Thirty-first Illinois on the right, close to Oglesby's left flank regiment, then the Twentieth, Forty-eighth, Forty-fifth, Forty-ninth, and Seventeenth Illinois. McAllister's battery was between the Eleventh and Twentieth, and Taylor's between the Seventeenth and Forty-ninth. Colonel Dickey's cavalry was in rear, his horses picketed in the woods and eating corn. North of the Fort Henry road was Colonel Cruft's brigade of General Lewis Wallace's division, the Twenty-fifth Kentucky having the right, then the Thirty-first Indiana, the Seventeenth Kentucky, the Forty-fourth Indiana, with Wood's battery.

These are all the regiments which took part in the terrible fight of Saturday forenoon. They were unprepared for the assault. The soldiers had not risen from their snowy beds. The reveille was just sounding when the sharp crack of the rifles was heard in the thickets on the extreme right. Then the artillery opened. Schwartz's, Dresser's, McAllister's, and Taylor's men sprang from their blankets to their guns. It was hardly light enough to see the enemy. They could only distinguish the flashes of the guns and the wreaths of smoke through the branches of the trees; but they aimed at the flashes, and sent their shells upon the advancing columns.

The Rebel batteries replied, and the wild uproar of the terrible day began.

Instead of moving west, directly upon the front of Oglesby, McArthur, and Wallace, the Rebel column under Pillow marched down the Union Ferry road south a half-mile, then turned abruptly towards the northwest. You see by the accompanying diagram how the troops stood at the beginning of the battle. There is McArthur's brigade with Schwartz's battery, Oglesby's brigade with Dresser's battery, Wallace's brigade with McAllister's and Taylor's batteries,—all facing the town. Across the brook, upon the north side of the ravine, is Cruft's brigade. You see Pillow's brigades wheeling upon McArthur and Oglesby, and across the Fort Henry road, coming down from the breastworks, are General Buckner's brigades.

Schwartz, Dresser, and McAllister wheel their guns towards Pillow's column. The Rebels open with a volley of musketry. The fire is aimed at the Eighth and Twenty-ninth Illinois regiments, which, you remember, are on the right of Oglesby's brigade. The men are cold. They have sprung from their icy beds to take their places in the ranks. They have a scant supply of ammunition, and are unprepared for the assault, but they are not the men to run at the first fire. The Rebel musketry begins to thin their ranks, but they do not flinch. They send their volleys into the face of the enemy.

Another Rebel brigade arrives, and fires upon the Thirtieth and Thirty-first Illinois,—the two regiments on the left of Oglesby's brigade. Colonel John A. Logan commands the Thirty-first. He told the Southern conspirators in Congress, when they were about to secede from the Union, that the men of the Northwest would hew their way to the Gulf of Mexico with their swords, if they attempted to close the Mississippi. He is not disposed to yield his ground. He encourages his men, and they remain immovable before the Rebel

71

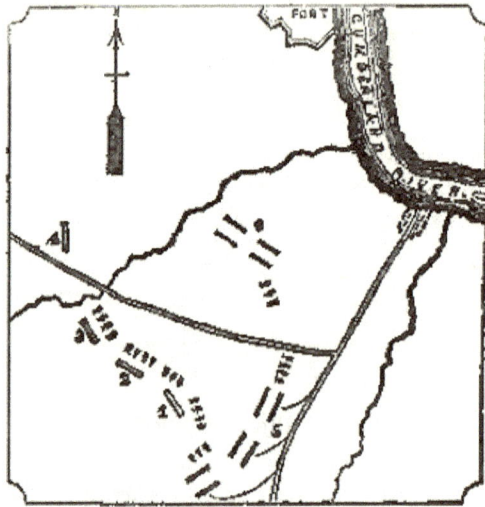

THE ATTACK ON McCLERNAND.

| | |
|---|---|
| 1 McArthur's brigade. | 4 Cruft's brigade. |
| 2 Oglesby's brigade. | 5 Pillow's divisions. |
| 3 W. H. L. Wallace's brigade. | 6 Buckner's divisions. |

brigades. Instead of falling back, he swings his regiment towards the Rebels, and stands confronting them.

But while this is going on, the Rebel cavalry have moved round to the rear of McArthur. They dash down a ravine, through the bushes, over the fallen trees, and charge up the hill upon the Ninth and Eighteenth regiments of McArthur's brigade. They are sent back in confusion, but the onset has been so fierce and the charge so far in the rear, that McArthur is compelled to fall back and form a new line. The Rebels have begun to open the door which General Grant had closed against them. The brigades in front of Oglesby are pouring murderous volleys upon the Eighth and Twenty-ninth. The falling back of McArthur to meet the attack on his rear has enabled the enemy to come up behind these regiments, and they are also compelled to fall back.

The Rebels in front are elated. They move nearer, working their way along a ravine, sheltered by a ridge of land. They load their muskets, rush up to the crest of the hill, deliver their fire, and step back to reload; but as often as they appear, McAllister and Dresser and Taylor give them grape and canister.

The Eleventh and Twentieth Illinois, on the right of Wallace's brigade, join in the conflict, supporting the brave Logan. Colonel Wallace swings the Forty-eighth, Forty-fifth, and half of the Forty-ninth round towards Pillow's brigades, leaving the other half of the Forty-ninth and the Seventeenth to hold the line towards the Fort Henry road. If you study the diagram carefully, you will see that this manoeuvre was a change of front. At the beginning the line of battle faced northeast, but now it faces south.

There is a ridge between Wallace's brigade and the Rebels. As often as the Rebels advance to the ridge, Taylor and McAllister with the infantry drive them back. It is an obstinate and bloody contest. The snow becomes crimson. There are pools of clotted blood where the brave men lie down upon the ground. There are bayonet-charges, fierce hand-to-hand contests. The Rebels rush upon McAllister's guns, but are turned back. The lines surge to and fro like the waves of the sea. The dying and the dead are trampled beneath the feet of the contending hosts.

Wallace hears a sharp fire in his rear. The Rebels have pushed out once more towards the west and are coming in again upon the right flank of the new battle line. McClernand sees that he is contending against overwhelming numbers, and he sends a messenger in haste to General Lewis Wallace, who sends Cruft's brigade to his assistance. The brigade goes down the road upon the run. The soldiers shout and hurrah. They pass in rear of Taylor's battery, and push on to the right to help Oglesby and McArthur.

The Rebels have driven those brigades. The men are hastening to the rear with doleful stories. Some of them rush through Cruft's brigade. Cruft meets the advancing Rebels face to face. The din of battle has lulled for a moment, but now it rolls again louder than before. The Rebels dash on, but it is like the dashing of the waves against a rock. Cruft's men are unmoved, though the Rebels advance till they are within twenty feet of the line. There are deafening volleys. The smoke from the opposing lines becomes a single cloud. The Rebels are held in check on the right by their firmness and endurance.

But just at this moment General Buckner's brigades come out of their entrenchments. They pass in front of their rifle-pits at the base of the hill, and march rapidly down to the Dover road. Colonel Wallace sees them. In a few minutes they will pour their volleys into the backs of his men. You remember that the Seventeenth and part of the Forty-ninth Illinois regiments were left standing near the road. You hear from their muskets now. They stand their ground and meet the onset manfully. Two guns of Taylor's battery, which have been thundering towards the south, wheel round to the northeast and sweep the Rebels with grape and canister.

Three fourths of the Rebel army is pressing upon McClernand's one division. His troops are disappearing. Hundreds are killed and wounded. Men who carry the wounded to rear do not return. The Rebels see their advantage, and charge upon Schwartz's and McAllister's batteries, but are repulsed. Reinforced by new regiments, they rush on again. They shoot the gunners and the horses and seize the cannon. The struggle is fierce, but unequal. Oglesby's men are overpowered, the line gives way. The Rebels push on with a yell, and seize several of Schwartz's and McAllister's guns. The gunners fight determinedly for a moment, but they are few against many, and are shot or taken prisoners. A Mississippi regiment attempts to capture Taylor's guns, but he sweeps it back with grape and canister.

Up to this moment Wallace has not yielded an inch. Two of Oglesby's regiments next to his brigade still hold their ground, but all who stood beyond are in full retreat. The Rebels have picked off a score of brave officers in Oglesby's command,—Colonels Logan, Lawler, and Ransom are wounded. Lieutenant-Colonel White of the Thirty-first, Lieutenant-Colonel Smith of the Forty-eighth, Lieutenant-Colonel Irvin of the Twentieth, and Major Post of the Eighth are killed. The men of Oglesby's brigade, although they have lost so many of their leaders, are not panic-stricken. They are overpowered for the moment. Some of the regiments are out of ammunition. They know that reinforcements are at hand, and they fall back in order.

To understand Wallace's position at this stage of the battle, imagine that you stand with your face towards the south fighting a powerful antagonist, that a second equally powerful is coming up on your right hand, and that a third is giving heavy blows upon your left shoulder, almost in your back. Pillow, with one half of his brigades, is in front, Johnson, with the other half of Pillow's command, is coming up on the right, and Buckner, with all of his brigades, is moving down upon the left.

Wallace sees that he must retreat. The Eleventh and Thirty-first—Ransom's and Logan's regiments—are still fighting on Wallace's right. There is great slaughter in their ranks, but they do not flee. They change front and march a few rods to the rear, come into line and fire a volley at the advancing Rebels. Forest's cavalry dashes upon them and cuts off a few prisoners, but the line is only bruised, not broken. Thus loading and firing, contesting all the ground, the troops descend the hill, cross the clear running brook, and march up the hill upon the other side.

But there are some frightened men, who fling away their guns and rush wildly to the rear. An officer dashes down the road, crying: "We are cut to pieces! The day is lost!"

"Shut up your head, you scoundrel!" shouts General Wallace.

It has had an effect upon his troops. They are nervous, and look round, expecting to see the enemy in overwhelming numbers. General Wallace sees that there has been disaster. He does not wait for orders to march.

"Third brigade, by the right flank, double-quick, Forward, March!" Colonel Thayer commanding the brigade repeats the order. The men break into a run towards the front along the road. General Wallace gallops in advance, and meets Colonel Wallace conducting his brigade to the rear.

"We are out of ammunition. The enemy are following. If you will put your troops into line till we can fill our cartridge-boxes, we will stop them." He says it so coolly and deliberately that it astonishes General Wallace. It reassures him. He feels that it is a critical moment, but with men retiring so deliberately, there is no reason to be discouraged.

He leads Thayer's brigade up to the crest of the hill, just where the road begins to descend into the ravine, through which gurgles the clear running brook.

"Bring up Company A, Chicago Light Artillery!" he shouts to an aid. A few moments, and Captain Wood, who commands the battery, leads it along the road. The horses are upon the gallop. The teamsters lash them with their whips. They leap over logs, stones, stumps, and through the bushes. They halt at the crest of the hill.

"Put your guns here, two pieces in the road, and two on each side, and load with grape and canister."

The men spring to their pieces. They throw off their coats, and work in their shirt-sleeves. They ram home the cartridges and stand beside their pieces, waiting for the enemy.

The battery faces southeast. On the right of the battery, next to it, is the First Nebraska, and beyond it the Fifty-eighth Illinois. On the left of the battery is Captain Davison's company of the Thirty-second Illinois, and beyond it the Fifty-eighth Ohio. A few rods in rear is the Seventy-sixth Ohio and the Forty-sixth and Fifty-seventh Illinois.

McArthur, Oglesby, Wallace, and Cruft have all fallen back, and their regiments are reforming in the woods west of Thayer's position, and filling their cartridge-boxes.

The Rebels halt a little while upon the ground from which they have driven McClernand, rifling the pockets of the dead and robbing the wounded. General Pillow feels very well. He writes a despatch, which is telegraphed to Nashville,— *"On the honour of a soldier, the day is ours!"*

Buckner unites his brigades to Pillow's, and they prepare for a second advance. It gives General Wallace time to perfect his line. Willard's battery, which was left at Fort Henry, has just arrived. It gallops into position in the woods west of Thayer's brigade. Dresser and Taylor also come into position. They are ready.

The Rebels descend the hill on the east side of the brook, and move up the road. They are flushed with success, and are confident of defeating General Grant. General Floyd has changed his mind; instead of escaping, as he can do by the road leading to Nashville, he thinks he will put the army of General Grant to rout.

The advancing columns step across the brook, and begin to ascend the hill. The artillery opens its fire. The Rebel batteries reply. The infantry rolls its volleys. The hill and the hollow are enveloped in clouds of smoke. Wood's, Dresser's, Willard's, and Taylor's batteries open,—twenty-four guns send their grape and canister, shrapnel and shells, into the gray ranks which are vainly endeavouring to reach the top of the hill.

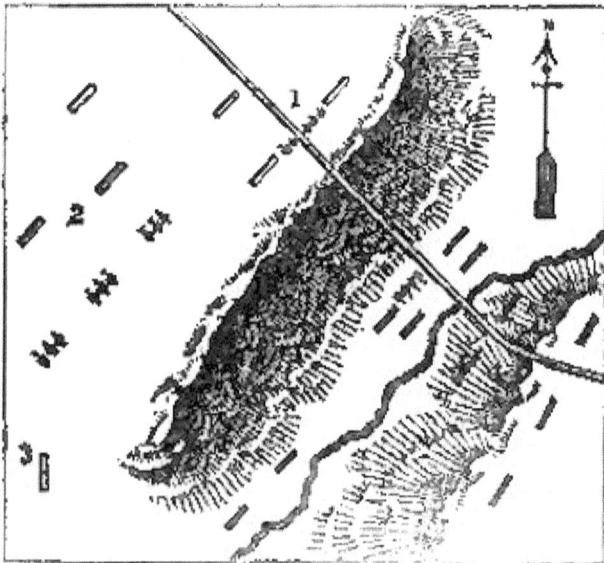

1 Thayer's brigade with Wood's battery.    3 Craft's brigade
2 McClernand's brigades.    4 Rebels.

The Rebels concentrate their fire upon Wood's battery and the First Nebraska, but those hardy pioneers from beyond the Missouri, some of them Rocky Mountain hunters, cannot be driven. The Rebels fire too high. The air is filled with the screaming of their bullets, and a wild storm sweeps over the heads of the men from Nebraska, who lose but ten men killed and wounded in this terrible contest. The Nebraska men are old hunters, and do not fire at random, but take deliberate aim.

The Rebels march half-way up the hill, and then fall back to the brook. They have lost courage. Their officers rally the wavering lines. Again they advance, but are forced back by the musketry and the grape and canister.

They break in confusion, and vain are all the attempts of the officers to rally them. General Floyd's plan, which worked so successfully in the morning, has failed at noon. General Pillow's telegram was sent too soon by a half-hour. The Rebels retire to the hill, and help themselves to the overcoats, blankets, beef, bread, and other things in McClernand's camp.

General Grant determined to assault the enemy's works. He thought that the rifle-pits at the northwest angle of the fort could be carried; that then he could plant his batteries so near that, under their fire, he could get into the fort. General Smith's division had not been engaged in the battles of the morning. His troops had heard the roar of the conflict and the cheers of their comrades when the Rebels were beaten back.

They were ready for action. They were nerved up to attempt great deeds for their country. The Rebels had been repulsed, and now they could defeat them.

General Grant directed General Wallace to move forward from his position, across the brook, drive the Rebels back, and then assault their works. A large body of Rebels still held the ground, from which McClernand had been driven.

General Wallace placed Colonel Morgan L. Smith's brigade in front. There was contention between the Eighth Missouri and Eleventh Indiana, for each wanted the honour of leading the assault. The Eleventh yielded to the Eighth, with the understanding that in the next assault it should have the advance. Thus with generous rivalry and unbounded enthusiasm they prepared to advance.

The Eleventh followed the Eighth. Colonel Cruft's brigade, with two Ohio regiments under Colonel Ross, completed the column. Colonel Cruft formed in line of battle to the right of Colonel Smith.

They crossed the brook. It was a dark and bloody ravine. The Rebel dead and wounded were lying there, thick almost as the withered forest-leaves. The snow was crimson. The brook was no longer a clear running stream, but red with blood.

General Wallace was aware of the desperate character of the enterprise. He told his men what they were to do,—to drive the enemy, and storm the breastworks.

"Hurrah! that's just what we want to do. Forward! Forward! We are ready!" were their answers. They could see the Rebel lines on the hill. The Rebels knew that they were to be attacked, and were ready to receive them.

Colonel Smith moved up the road. His point of attack was clear, but Cruft's was through brush and over stony ground. A line of skirmishers sprang out from the Eighth Missouri. They ran up the hill, and came face to face with the Rebel skirmishers.

They fought from tree to tree, firing, picking off an opponent, then falling upon the ground to reload.

The regiments followed. They were half-way up the hill, when a line of fire began to run round the crest.

"Down! down!" shouted Colonel Smith. The regiments fell flat, and the storm swept harmlessly over their heads. The Rebels cheered. They thought they had annihilated Colonel Smith's command. Up they rose, and rushed upon the enemy, pouring in their volleys, falling when the fight was hottest, rising as soon as the Rebels had fired. Thus they closed upon the enemy, and pushed him back over all the ground he had won in the morning, driving him into his works.

General Wallace was preparing to assault the works, when an officer dashed down the line with cheering news of success upon the left.

Returning now to General Smith's division, we see him preparing to storm the works near the northwest angle of the fort. Colonel Cook's brigade is directed to make a feint of attacking the fort. Major Cavender brings his heavy guns into position, and opens a furious cannonade, under cover of which Colonel Lauman is to advance upon the rifle-pits on the outer ridge. If he can get possession of those, Cavender can plant his guns there and rake the inner trenches.

Colonel Hanson's brigade,—the Second Kentucky, Twentieth Mississippi, and Thirtieth Tennessee, are in the rifle-pits. There are six pieces of artillery and another brigade behind the inner entrenchments, all ready to pour their fire upon the advancing columns. Colonel Hanson's men lie secure behind the trunks of the great forest oaks, their rifles thrust through between the logs. It is fifteen or twenty rods to the bottom of the slope, and there you find the fallen trees, with their branches interlocked, and sharp stakes driven into the ground. Beyond is the meadow where Lauman forms his brigade. The Rebels have a clear sweep of all the ground.

General Smith leads Lauman's men to the meadow, while Colonel Cook moves up on the left and commences the attack. The soldiers hear, far down on the right, Wallace's brigades driving the enemy from the hill. It is almost sunset. The rays of light fall aslant the meadow, upon the backs of Lauman's men, and into the faces of the Rebels. The advancing brigade is in solid column of regiments, the Second Iowa in front, then the Twenty-fifth Indiana, the Seventh and Fourteenth Iowa,—four firm, unwavering lines, which throw their shadows forward as they advance. Birges's sharpshooters, with their unerring rifles, are flung out on each flank.

The brigade halts upon the meadow. General Smith rides along the line, and informs them that they are to take the rifle-pits with the bayonet alone. He sits firmly on his horse, and his long gray hair, falling almost to his shoulders, waves in the evening breeze. He is an iron man, and he leads iron men. The Rebel cannon cut them through with solid

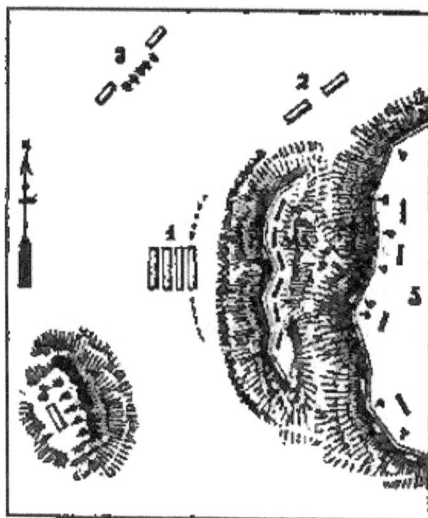

THE CHARGE OF LAUMAN'S BRIGADE.

1 Lauman's brigade.
2 Cook's brigade.
3 3 Cavender's batteries, with infantry.

4 Rebel rifle-pits.
5 Rebel inner works.

79

shot, shells burst above and around them, with loud explosions and terrifying shrieks from the flying fragments, men drop from the ranks, or are whirled into the air torn and mangled. There are sudden gaps, but not a man flinches. They look not towards the rear, but towards the front. There are the fallen trees, the hill, the line of two thousand muskets poised between the logs, the cannon thundering from the height beyond. There is no whispering in those solid ranks, no loud talking, nothing but the "Steady! steady!" of the officers. Their hearts beat great throbs. Their nerves are steel, their muscles iron. They grasp their muskets with the grip of tigers. Before them rides their General, his cap upon his sword, his long hair streaming like a banner in the wind. The colour-bearer, waving the stars and stripes, marches by his side.

They move across the meadow. All around them is the deafening roar of the conflict. Cavender is behind them, Cook is upon their left, the enemy is in front, and Wallace away upon their right. They reach the fallen trees at the foot of the hill. The pile of logs above them bursts into flame. A deadly storm, more terrible than the fiercest winter blast, sweeps down the slope into their faces. There are lightning flashes and thunderbolts from the hill above. Men drop from their places, to lie forever still among the tangled branches. But their surviving comrades do not falter. On,—on,—creeping, crawling, climbing over the obstructions, unterrified, undaunted, with all the energy of life centred in one effort; like a tornado they sweep up the slope,—into the line of fire, into the hissing storm, up to the logs, into the cloud, leaping like tigers, thrusting the bayonet home upon the foe. The Rebels reel, stagger, tumble, run!

"*Hurra—h!*"

It is a wild, prolonged, triumphant shout, like the blast of a trumpet. They plant their banners on the works, and fire their volleys into the retreating foe. Stone's battery gallops over the meadow, over the logs, up the hill, the horses leaping and plunging as if they, too, knew that victory was hanging in the scale. The gunners spring from their seats, wheel their pieces and throw their shells, an enfilading fire, into the upper works.

"Hurrah! hurrah! hurrah!" rings through the forest, down the line to Wallace's men.

"We have carried the works!" "We are inside!" shouts an officer bearing the welcome news.

The men toss their caps in the air. They shake hands, they shout, and break into singing. They forget all their hardships and sufferings, the hungry days, the horrible nights, the wounded and the dead. The success is worth all the sacrifice.

CHAPTER 6

# The Surrender

All through the night the brave men held the ground they had so nobly won. They rested on snowy beds. They had no supper. They could kindle no fires to warm the wintry air. The cannon above them hurled down shells, and sent volleys of grape, which screamed above and around them like the voices of demons in the darkness. The branches of the trees were torn from their trunks by the solid shot, and the trunks were splintered from top to bottom, but they did not falter or retire from that slope where the snow was crimsoned with the life-blood of hundreds of their comrades. Nearly four hundred had fallen in that attack. The hill had cost a great deal of blood, but it was worth all it cost, and they would not give it up. So they braved the leaden rain and iron hail through the weary hours of that winter night. They only waited for daybreak to storm the inner works and take the fort. Their ardour and enthusiasm was unbounded.

As the morning approached they heard a bugle-call. They looked across the narrow ravine, and saw, in the dim light of the dawn, a man waving a white flag upon the entrenchments. It was a sign for a parley. He jumped down from the embankment, and descended the hill.

"Halt! Who comes there?" shouted the picket.

"Flag of truce with a letter for General Grant."

An officer took the letter, and hastened down the slope, across the meadow, up to the house on the Dover road, where General Grant had his headquarters.

During the night there had been a council of war at General Floyd's headquarters. Nearly all the Rebel officers commanding brigades and regiments were there. They were down-hearted. They had fought bravely, won a victory, as they thought, but had lost it. A Rebel officer who was there told me what they said. General Floyd and

General Pillow blamed General Buckner for not advancing earlier in the morning, and for making what they thought a feeble attack. They could have escaped after they drove McClernand across the brook, but now they were hemmed in. The prospect was gloomy. The troops were exhausted by the long conflict, by constant watching, and by the cold. What bitter nights those were to the men who came from Texas, Alabama, and Mississippi, where the roses bloom and the blue-birds sing through all the winter months.

What should be done? Should they make another attack, and cut their way out, or should they surrender?

"I cannot hold my position a half-hour. The Yankees can turn my flank or advance directly upon the breastworks," said General Buckner.

"If you had advanced at the time agreed upon, and made a more vigorous attack, we should have routed the enemy," said General Floyd.

"I advanced as soon as I could, and my troops fought as bravely as others," was the response from General Buckner,—a middle-aged, medium-sized man. His hair is iron gray. He has thin whiskers and a moustache, and wears a gray kersey overcoat, with a great cape, and gold lace on the sleeves, and a black hat with a nodding black plume.

"Well, here we are, and it is useless to renew the attack with any hope of success. The men are exhausted," said General Floyd,—a stout, heavy man, with thick lips, a large nose, evil eyes, and coarse features.

"We can cut our way out," said Major Brown, commanding the Twentieth Mississippi,—a tall, black-haired, impetuous, fiery man.

"Some of us might escape in that way, but the attempt would be attended with great slaughter," responded General Floyd.

"My troops are so worn out and cut to pieces and demoralized, that I can't make another fight," said Buckner.

"My troops will fight till they die," answered Major Brown, setting his teeth together.

"It will cost the command three quarters of its present number to cut its way through, and it is wrong to sacrifice three quarters of a command to save the other quarter," Buckner continued.

"No officer has a right to cause such a sacrifice," said Major Gilmer, of General Pillow's staff.

"But we can hold out another day, and by that time we can get steamboats here to take us across the river," said General Pillow.

"No, I can't hold my position a half-hour, and the Yankees will renew the attack at daybreak," Buckner replied.

"Then we have got to surrender, for aught I see," said an officer.

"I won't surrender the command, neither will I be taken prisoner," said Floyd. He doubtless remembered how he had stolen public property, while in office under Buchanan, and would rather die than to fall into the hands of those whom he knew would be likely to bring him to an account for his villainy.

"I don't intend to be taken prisoner," said Pillow.

"What will you do, gentlemen?" Buckner asked.

"I mean to escape, and take my Virginia brigade with me, if I can. I shall turn over the command to General Pillow. I have a right to escape if I can, but I haven't any right to order the entire army to make a hopeless fight," said Floyd.

"If you surrender it to me, I shall turn it over to General Buckner," said General Pillow, who was also disposed to shirk responsibility and desert the men whom he had induced to vote to secede from the Union and take up arms against their country.

"If the command comes into my hands, I shall deem it my duty to surrender it. I shall not call upon the troops to make a useless sacrifice of life, and I will not desert the men who have fought so nobly," Buckner replied, with a bitterness which made Floyd and Pillow wince.

It was past midnight. The council broke up. The brigade and regimental officers were astonished at the result. Some of them broke out into horrid cursing and swearing at Floyd and Pillow.

"It is mean!"

"It is cowardly!"

"Floyd always was a rascal."

"We are betrayed!" "There is treachery!" said they.

"It is a mean trick for an officer to desert his men. If my troops are to be surrendered, I shall stick by them," said Major Brown.

"I denounce Pillow as a coward, and if I ever meet him, I'll shoot him as quick as I would a dog," said Major McLain, red with rage.

Floyd gave out that he was going to join Colonel Forrest, who commanded the cavalry, and thus cut his way out; but there were two or three small steamboats at the Dover landing. He and General Pillow jumped on board one of them, and then secretly marched a portion of the Virginia brigade on board. Other soldiers saw what was going on, that they were being deserted. They became frantic with terror and rage. They rushed on board, crowding every part of the boat.

"Cut loose!" shouted Floyd to the captain. The boats swung into the stream and moved up the river, leaving thousands of infuriated soldiers on the landing. So the man who had stolen the public property, and who did all he could to bring on the war, who induced thousands of poor, ignorant men to take up arms, deserted his post, stole away in the darkness, and left them to their fate.

General Buckner immediately wrote a letter to General Grant, asking for an armistice till twelve o'clock, and the appointment of commissioners to agree upon terms by which the fort and the prisoners should be surrendered.

"No terms, other than unconditional and immediate surrender can be accepted. I propose to move immediately upon your works," was General Grant's reply.

General Buckner replied, that he thought it very *unchivalrous*, but accepted the terms. He meant that he did not think it very honourable in General Grant to require an unconditional surrender. He professed to have a high sense of all that was noble, generous, honourable, and high-minded. But a few days before he had so forgotten those qualities of character, that he took some cattle from Rev. Mr. Wiggin of Rochester, Kentucky, one of his old acquaintances, and paid him with a check of three hundred dollars on the Southern Bank at Russelville. When Rev. Mr. Wiggin called at the bank and presented the check, the cashier told him that General Buckner never had had any money on deposit there, and the bank did not owe him a dollar! He cheated and swindled the minister, and committed the crime of forgery, which would have sent him to the state-prison in time of peace.

The morning dawned,—Sunday morning, calm, clear, and beautiful. The horrible nights were over and the freezing days gone by. The air was mild, and there was a gentle breeze from the south, which brought the blue-birds. They did not mind the soldiers or the cannon, but chirped and sang in the woods as merrily as ever.

I saw the white flag flying on the breastworks. The soldiers and sailors saw it, and cheered. General Grant had moved his headquarters to the steamboat Uncle Sam, and, as I happened to be on board that boat, I saw a great deal that took place.

The gunboats, and all the steamboats, fifty or more, began to move up the river. Dense clouds of smoke rolled up from the tall chimneys. The great wheels plashed the sparkling stream. Flags were flying on all the staffs. The army began its march into the fort. The bands played. How grand the crash of the drums and the trumpets! The soldiers marched proudly. The columns were winding along the hills,—the artillery, the infantry, the cavalry, with all their banners waving, and

84

the bright sunshine gleaming and glistening on their bayonets! They entered the fort, and planted their standards on the embankments. The gunboats and the field artillery fired a grand salute. From the steamboats, from the hillside, from the fort, and the forest there were answering shouts. The wounded in the hospitals forgot, for the moment, that they were torn and mangled, raised themselves on their beds of straw, and mingled their feeble cheers in the universal rejoicing!

Thirteen thousand men, sixty-seven pieces of artillery, and fifteen thousand small arms were surrendered. A motley, care-worn, haggard, anxious crowd stood at the landing. I sprang ashore, and walked through the ranks. Some were standing, some lying down, taking no notice of what was going on around them. They were prisoners of war. When they joined the army, they probably did not dream that they would be taken prisoners. They were to be victorious, and capture the Yankees. They were poor, ignorant men. Not half of them knew how to read or write. They had been deluded by their leaders,—the slaveholders. They had fought bravely, but they had been defeated, and their generals had deserted them. No wonder they were down-hearted.

Their clothes were of all colours. Some wore gray, some blue, some butternut-coloured clothes,—a dirty brown. They were very ragged. Some had old quilts for blankets, others faded pieces of carpeting, others strips of new carpeting, which they had taken from the stores. Some had caps, others old slouched felt hats, and others nothing but straw hats upon their heads.

"We fought well, but you outnumbered us," said one.

"We should have beaten you as it was, if it hadn't been for your gunboats," said another.

"How happened it that General Floyd and General Pillow escaped, and left you?" I asked.

"They are traitors. I would shoot the scoundrels, if I could get a chance," said a fellow in a snuff-coloured coat, clenching his fist.

"I am glad the fighting is over. I don't want to see another such day as yesterday," said a Tennessean, who was lying on the ground.

"What will General Grant do with us? Will he put us in prison?" asked one.

"That will depend upon how you behave. If you had not taken up arms against your country, you would not have been in trouble now."

"We couldn't help it, sir. I was forced into the army, and I am glad I am a prisoner. I sha'n't have to fight any more," said a blue-eyed young man, not more than eighteen years old.

There were some who were very sullen and sour, and there were others who did not care what became of them.

I went up the hill into the town. Nearly every house was filled with the dying and the dead. The shells from the gunboats had crashed through some of the buildings. The soldiers had cut down the orchards and the shade-trees, and burned the fences. All was desolation. There were sad groups around the camp-fires, with despair upon their countenances. O how many of them thought of their friends far away, and wished they could see them again!

The ground was strewed with their guns, cartridge-boxes, belts, and knapsacks. There were bags of corn, barrels of sugar, hogsheads of molasses, tierces of bacon, broken open and trodden into the mud.

I went into the fort, and saw where the great shells from the gunboats had cut through the embankments. There were piles of cartridges beside the cannon. The dead were lying there, torn, mangled, rent. Near the entrenchments, where the fight had been fiercest, there were pools of blood. The Rebel soldiers were breaking the frozen earth, digging burial-trenches, and bringing in their fallen comrades and laying them side by side, to their last, long, silent sleep. I looked down the slope where Lauman's men swept over the fallen trees in their terrible charge; then I walked down to the meadow, and looked up the height, and wondered how men could climb over the trees, the stumps, the rocks, and ascend it through such a storm. The dead were lying where they fell, heroes every one of them! It was sad to think that so many noble men had fallen, but it was a pleasure to know that they had not faltered. They had done their duty. If you ever visit that battle-field, and stand upon that slope, you will feel your heart swell with gratitude and joy, to think how cheerfully they gave their lives to save their country, that you and all who come after you may enjoy peace and prosperity forever.

How bravely they fought! There, upon the cold ground, lay a soldier of the Ninth Illinois. Early in the action of Saturday he was shot through the arm. He went to the hospital and had it bandaged, and returned to his place in the regiment. A second shot passed through his thigh, tearing the flesh to shreds.

"We will carry you to the hospital," said two of his comrades.

"No, you stay and fight. I can get along alone." He took off his bayonet, used his gun for a crutch, and reached the hospital. The surgeon dressed the wound. He heard the roar of battle. His soul was on fire to be there. He hobbled once more to the field, and went into the thickest of the fight, lying down, because he could not stand. He fought as a skirmisher. When the Rebels advanced, he could not retire with the troops, but continued to fight. After the battle he was found dead upon the field, six bullets having passed through his body.

One bright-eyed little fellow, of the Second Iowa, had his foot crushed by a cannon-shot. Two of his comrades carried him to the rear. An officer saw that, unless the blood was stopped, he never would reach the hospital. He told the men to tie a handkerchief around his leg, and put snow on the wound.

"O, never mind the foot, Captain," said the brave fellow. "We drove the Rebels out, and have got their trench; that's the most I care for!"

The soldiers did as they were directed, and his life was saved.

There in the trenches was a Rebel soldier with a rifle-shot through his head. He was an excellent marksman, and had killed or wounded several Union officers. One of Colonel Birges's sharpshooters, an old hunter, who had killed many bears and wolves, crept up towards the breastworks to try his hand upon the Rebel. They fired at each other again and again, but both were shrewd and careful. The Rebel raised his hat above the breastwork,—*whi*—*z!* The sharpshooter out in the bushes had put a bullet through it. "*Ha! ha! ha!*" laughed the Rebel, sending his own bullet into the little puff of smoke down in the ravine. The Rocky Mountain hunter was as still as a mouse. He knew that the Rebel had outwitted him, and expected the return shot. It was aimed a little too high, and he was safe.

"You cheated me that time, but I will be even with you yet," said the sharpshooter, whirling upon his back, and loading his rifle and whirling back again. He rested his rifle upon the ground, aimed it, and lay with his eye along the barrel, his finger on the trigger. Five minutes passed. "I reckon that that last shot fixed him," said the Rebel. "He hasn't moved this five minutes."

He raised his head, peeped over the embankment, and fell back lifeless. The unerring rifle-bullet had passed through his head.

If you could go over the battle-ground with one of those sharp-shooters, he would show you a little clump of bushes, and some stumps, where three or four of them lay on Saturday, in front of one of the Rebel batteries, and picked off the gunners. Two or three times the artillerymen tried to drive them out with shells; but they lay close upon the ground, and the shells did not touch them. The artillerymen were obliged to cease firing, and retreat out of reach of the deadly bullets.

Some of the Rebel officers took their surrender very much to heart. They were proud, insolent, and defiant. Their surrender was unconditional, and they thought it very hard to give up their swords and pistols. One of them fired a pistol at Major Mudd, of the Second Illinois, wounding him in the back. I was very well acquainted with the Major. He lived in St. Louis, and had been from the beginning an ardent friend of the Union. He had hunted the guerrillas in Missouri, and had fought bravely at Wilson's Creek. It is quite likely he was shot by an old enemy. General Grant at once issued orders that all the Rebel officers should be disarmed. General Buckner, in insolent tones, said to General Grant that it was barbarous, inhuman, brutal, unchivalrous, and at variance with the rules of civilized warfare! General Grant replied:

"You have dared to come here to complain of my acts, without the right to make an objection. You do not appear to remember that your surrender was unconditional. Yet, if we compare the acts of the different armies in this war, how will yours bear inspection? You have cowardly shot my officers in cold blood. As I rode over the field, I saw the dead of my army brutally insulted by your men, their clothing stripped off of them, and their bodies exposed, without the slightest regard for common decency. Humanity has seldom marked your course whenever our men have been unfortunate enough to fall into your hands. At Belmont your authorities disregarded all the usages of civilized warfare. My officers were crowded into cotton-pens with my brave soldiers, and then thrust into prison, while your officers were permitted to enjoy their parole, and live at the hotel in Cairo. Your men are given the same fare as my own, and your wounded receive our best attention. These are incontrovertible facts. I have simply taken the precaution to disarm your officers and men, because necessity compelled me to protect my own from assassination."

General Buckner had no reply to make. He hung his head in shame at the rebuke.

Major Mudd, though severely wounded, recovered, but lost his life in another battle. One day, while riding with him in Missouri, he told me a very good story. He said he was once riding in the cars, and that a very inquisitive man sat by his side. A few rods from every road-crossing the railroad company had put up boards with the letters W. R. upon them.

"What be them for?" asked the man.

"Those are directions to the engineer to blow the whistle and ring the bell, that people who may be on the carriage-road may look out and not get run over by the train," the Major answered.

"O yes, I see."

The man sat in silence awhile, with his lips working as if he was trying to spell.

"Well, Major," he said at last, "it may be as you say. I know that *w-r-i-n-g* spells ring, but for the life of me I don't see how you can get an R into whistle!"

The fall of Fort Donelson was a severe blow to the Rebels. It had a great effect. It was the first great victory of the Union troops. It opened all the northwest corner of the Confederacy. It compelled General Johnston to retreat from Bowling Green, and also compelled the evacuation of Columbus and all Central Tennessee. Nashville, the capital of that State, fell into the hands of the Union troops.

On Sunday morning the Rebels at Nashville were in good spirits. General Pillow had telegraphed on Saturday noon, as you remember, "On the honour of a soldier, the day is ours." The citizens shouted over it.

One sober citizen said: "I never liked Pillow, but I forgive him now. He is the man for the occasion."

Another, who had been Governor of the State,—a wicked, profane man,—said: "It is first-rate news. Pillow is giving the Yankees hell, and rubbing it in!"[6] It is a vile sentence, and I would not quote it, were it not that you might have a true picture from Rebel sources.

The newspapers put out bulletins:

*Enemy Retreating!*

*Glorious Result!!*

*Our Boys Following and Peppering Their Rear!!*

*A Complete Victory!*

The bell-ringers rang jubilant peals, and the citizens shook hands over the good news as they went to church. Services had hardly commenced, when a horseman dashed through the streets, covered with mud, and almost breathless from hard riding, shouting, "Fort Donelson has surrendered, and the Yankees are coming!"

The people poured out from the churches and their houses into the street. Such hurrying to and fro was never seen. Men, women, and children ran here and there, not knowing what to do, imagin-

---

6: *Mobile Tribune.*

ing that the Yankees would murder them. They began to pack their goods. Carts, wagons, carriages, drays, wheelbarrows,—all were loaded. Strong men were pale with fear, women wrung their hands, and children cried.

Before noon Generals Floyd and Pillow arrived on steamboats. The people crowded round the renegade officers, and called for a speech. General Floyd went out upon the balcony of the hotel, and said:

"Fellow-Citizens: This is not the time for speaking, but for action. It is a time when every man should enlist for the war. Not a day is to be lost. We had only ten thousand effective men, who fought four days and nights against forty thousand of the enemy. But nature could hold out no longer. The men required rest, and having lost one third of my gallant force I was compelled to retire. We have left a thousand of the enemy dead on the field. General Johnston has not slept a wink for three nights; he is all worn out, but he is acting wisely. He is going to entice the Yankees into the mountain gaps, away from the rivers and the gunboats, and then drive them back, and carry the war into the enemy's country."[7]

General Johnston's army, retreating from Bowling Green, began to pass through the city. The soldiers did not stop, but passed on towards the South. The people had thought that General Johnston would defend the place, the capital of the State; but when they saw that the troops were retreating, they recklessly abandoned their homes. It was a wild night in Nashville. The Rebels had two gunboats nearly completed, which were set on fire. The Rebel storehouses were thrown open to the poor people, who rushed pell-mell to help themselves to pork, flour, molasses, and sugar. A great deal was destroyed. After Johnston's army had crossed the river, the beautiful and costly wire suspension bridge which spanned it was cut down. It cost two hundred and fifty thousand dollars, and belonged to the daughters of the Rebel General Zollicoffer, who was killed at the battle of Mill Springs in Kentucky. The Rebel officers undertook to carry off the immense supplies of food which had been accumulated; but in the panic, barrels of meat and flour, sacks of coffee, hogsheads of sugar were rolled into the streets and trampled into the mire. Millions of dollars' worth were lost to the Confederacy. The farmers in the country feared that they would lose their slaves, and from all the section round they hurried the poor creatures towards the South, hoping to find a place where they would be secure.

---

7: *Lynchburg Republican.*

Throughout the South there was gloom and despondency. But all over the North there was great rejoicing. Everybody praised the brave soldiers who had fought so nobly. There were public meetings, speeches, processions, illuminations and bonfires, and devout thanksgivings to God.

The deeds of the brave men of the West were praised in poetry and song. Some stanzas were published in the *Atlantic Monthly* in Boston, which are so beautiful that I think you will thank me for quoting them.

*O gales that dash the Atlantic's swell*
*Along our rocky shores,*
*Whose thunders diapason well*
*New England's glad hurrahs,*

*Bear to the prairies of the West*
*The echoes of our joy,*
*The prayer that springs in every breast,—*
*'God bless thee, Illinois!'*

*O awful hours, when grape and shell*
*Tore through the unflinching line!*
*'Stand firm! remove the men who fell!*
*Close up, and wait the sign.'*

*It came at last, 'Now, lads, the steel!'*
*The rushing hosts deploy;*
*'Charge, boys!'—the broken traitors reel,—*
*Huzza for Illinois!*

*In vain thy rampart, Donelson,*
*The living torrent bars,*
*It leaps the wall, the fort is won,*
*Up go the Stripes and Stars.*

*Thy proudest mother's eyelids fill,*
*As dares her gallant boy,*
*And Plymouth Rock and Bunker Hill*
*Yearn to thee, Illinois.*

CHAPTER 7

# The Army at Pittsburg Landing

On the 6th and 7th of April, 1862, one of the greatest battles of the war was fought near Pittsburg Landing in Tennessee, on the west bank of the Tennessee River, about twelve miles from the northeast corner of the State of Mississippi. The Rebels call it the battle of Shiloh, because it was fought near Shiloh Church. I did not see the terrible contest, but I reached the place soon after the fight, in season to see the guns, cannon, wagons, knapsacks, cartridge-boxes, which were scattered over the ground, and the newly-made graves where the dead had just been buried. I was in camp upon the field several weeks, and saw the woods, the plains, hills, ravines. Officers and men who were in the fight pointed out the places where they stood, showed me where the Rebels advanced, where their batteries were, how they advanced and retreated, how the tide of victory ebbed and flowed. Having been so early on the ground, and having listened to the stories of a great many persons, I shall try to give you a correct account. It will be a difficult task, however, for the stories are conflicting. No two persons see a battle alike; each has his own standpoint. He sees what takes place around him. No other one will tell a story like his. Men have different temperaments. One is excited, and another is cool and collected. Men live fast in battle. Every nerve is excited, every sense intensified, and it is only by taking the accounts of different observers that an accurate view can be obtained.

After the capture of Fort Donelson, you remember that General Johnston retreated through Nashville towards the South. A few days later the Rebels evacuated Columbus on the Mississippi. They were obliged to concentrate their forces. They saw that Memphis would be the next point of attack, and they must defend it. All of their energies were aroused. The defeat of the Union army at Bull Run, you remember, caused a great uprising of the North, and so the fall of Donelson stirred the people of the South.

If you look at the map of Tennessee, you will notice, about twenty miles from Pittsburg Landing, the town of Corinth. It is at the junction of the Memphis and Charleston and the Mobile and Ohio Railroads, which made it an important place to the Rebels.

"Corinth must be defended," said the Memphis newspapers.

Governor Harris of Tennessee issued a proclamation calling upon the people to enlist.

> As Governor of your State, and Commander-in-Chief of its army, I call upon every able-bodied man of the State, without regard to age, to enlist in its service. I command him who can obtain a weapon to march with our armies. I ask him who can repair or forge an arm to make it ready at once for the soldier.

General Beauregard was sent in great haste to the West by Jeff Davis, who hoped that the fame and glory which he had won by attacking Fort Sumter and at Bull Run would rouse the people of the Southwest and save the failing fortunes of the Confederacy.

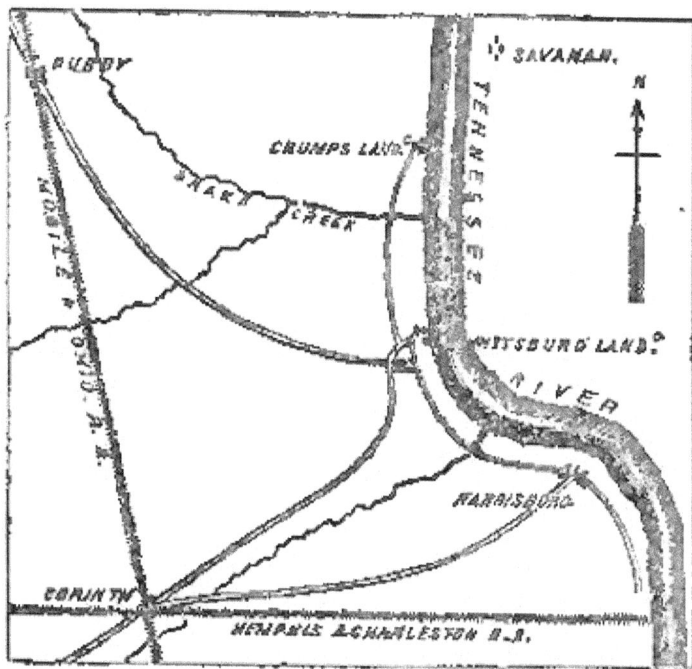

PITTSBURG LANDING AND VICINITY.

To Corinth came the flower of the Southern army. All other points were weakened to save Corinth. From Pensacola came General Bragg and ten thousand Alabamians, who had watched for many months the little frowning fortress on Santa Rosa Island. The troops which had been at Mobile to resist the landing of General Butler from Ship Island were hastened north upon the trains of the Mobile and Ohio road. General Beauregard called upon the Governors of Tennessee, Mississippi, Alabama, and Louisiana for additional troops.

General Polk, who had been a bishop before the war, sent down two divisions from Columbus on the Mississippi. General Johnston with his retreating army hastened on, and thus all the Rebel troops in the South-western States were mustered at Corinth.

The call to take up arms was responded to everywhere; old men and boys came trooping into the place. They came from Texas, Arkansas, and Missouri. Beauregard laboured with unremitting energy to create an army which would be powerful enough to drive back the Union troops, recover Tennessee, and invade Kentucky.

General Grant, after the capture of Donelson, moved his army, on steamboats, down the Cumberland and up the Tennessee, to Pittsburg Landing. He made his headquarters at Savannah, a small town ten miles below Pittsburg Landing, on the east side of the river.

General Buell, who had followed General Johnston through Nashville with the army of the Ohio, was slowly making his way across the country to join General Grant. The Rebel generals had the railroads, by which they could rapidly concentrate their troops, and they determined to attack General Grant at Pittsburg, with their superior force, before General Buell could join him. Beauregard had his pickets within four miles of General Grant's force, and he could move his entire army within striking distance before General Grant would know of his danger. He calculated that he could annihilate General Grant, drive him into the river, or force him to surrender, capture all of his cannon, wagons, ammunition, provisions, steamboats,—everything,—by a sudden stroke. If he succeeded, he could then move against General Buell, destroy his army, and not only recover all that had been lost, but he would also redeem Kentucky and invade Ohio, Indiana, and Illinois.

All but one division of General Grant's army was at Pittsburg. Two miles above the Landing the river begins to make its great eastern bend. Lick Creek comes in from the west, at the bend. Three miles below Pittsburg is Snake Creek, which also comes in from the west.

Five miles further down is Crump's Landing. General Lewis Wallace's division was near Crump's, but the other divisions were between the two creeks. The banks of the river are seventy-five feet high, and the country is a succession of wooded hills, with numerous ravines. There are a few clearings and farm-houses, but it is nearly all forest,—tall oak-trees, with here and there thickets of underbrush. The farmers cultivate a little corn, cotton, and tobacco. The country has been settled many years, but is almost as wild as when the Indians possessed the land.

Pittsburg is the nearest point to Corinth on the river. The road from the Landing winds up the bank, passes along the edge of a deep ravine, and leads southwest. As you go up the road, you come to a log-cabin about a mile from the river. There is a peach-orchard near by. There the roads fork. The left-hand road takes you to Hamburg, the middle one is the Ridge road to Corinth, and the third is the road to Shiloh Church, called also the Lower Corinth road. There are other openings in the woods,—old cotton-fields. Three miles out from the river you come to Shiloh Church. A clear brook, which is fed by springs, gurgles over a sandy bed, close by the church. You fill your canteen, and find it excellent water. On Sunday noons, the people who come to church sit down beneath the grand old trees, eat their dinners, and drink from the brook.

It is not such a church as you see in your own village. It has no tall steeple or tapering spire, no deep-toned bell, no organ, no singing-seats or gallery, no pews or carpeted aisles. It is built of logs. It was chinked with clay years ago, but the rains have washed it out. You can thrust your hand between the cracks. It is thirty or forty feet square. It has places for windows, but there are no sashes, and of course no glass. As you stand within, you can see up to the roof, supported by hewn rafters, and covered with split shingles, which shake and rattle when the wind blows. It is the best-ventilated church you ever saw. It has no pews, but only rough seats for the congregation. A great many of the churches of this section of the country are no better than this. Slavery does not build neat churches and school-houses, as a general thing. Around this church the battle raged fearfully.

Not far from the church, a road leads northeast towards Crump's Landing, and another northwest towards the town of Purdy. By the church, along the road leading down to the Landing, at the peach-orchard, and in the ravines you find the battle-ground.

General Johnston was senior commander of the Rebel army. He had Beauregard, Bragg, Polk, Hardee, Cheatham,—all Major-Generals, who had been educated at West Point, at the expense of the United States. They were considered to be the ablest generals in the Rebel service. General Breckenridge was there. He was Vice-President under Buchanan, and was but a few weeks out of his seat in the Senate of the United States. He was, you remember, the slaveholders' candidate for President in 1860. Quite likely he felt very sour against the Northern people, because he was not elected President.

The Rebel army numbered between forty and fifty thousand men. General Johnston worked with all his might to organize into brigades the troops which were flocking in from all quarters. It was of the utmost importance that the attack should be made before General Buell joined General Grant. The united and concentrated forces of Beauregard, Bragg, and Johnston outnumbered Grant's army by fifteen thousand. General Van Dorn, with thirty thousand men, was expected from Arkansas. They were to come by steamboat to Memphis, and were to be transported to Corinth by the Memphis and Charleston Railroad; but Van Dorn was behind time, and, unless the attack was made at once, it would be too late, for the combined armies of Grant and Buell would outnumber the Rebels. At midnight, on the 1st of April, Johnston learned that General Buell's advance divisions were within two or three days' march of Savannah. He immediately issued his orders to his corps commanders, directing the routes which each was to take in advancing towards Pittsburg.

The troops began their march on Thursday morning. They were in excellent spirits. They cheered, swung their hats, and marched with great enthusiasm. The Rebel officers, who knew the situation, the ground where General Grant was encamped, believed that his army would be annihilated. They assured the troops it would be a great and glorious victory.

The distance was only eighteen miles, and General Johnston intended to strike the blow at daylight on Saturday morning, but it rained hard Friday night, and the roads in the morning were so muddy that the artillery could not move. It was late Saturday afternoon before his army was in position. It was too near night to make the attack. He examined the ground, distributed ammunition, posted the artillery, gave the men extra rations, and waited for Sunday morning.

The Union army rested in security. No entrenchments were thrown up on the hills and along the ridges. No precautions were taken against surprise. The officers and soldiers did not dream of being attacked. They were unprepared. The divisions were not in order for battle. They were preparing to advance upon Corinth, and were to march when General Halleck, who was at St. Louis, commanding the department, should take the field.

On the evening of Friday the pickets on the Corinth road, two miles out from Shiloh Church, were fired upon. A body of Rebels rushed through the woods, and captured several officers and men. The Seventieth, Seventy-second, and Forty-eighth Ohio, of General Sherman's division, were sent out upon a reconnaissance. They came upon a couple of Rebel regiments, and, after a sharp action, drove them back to a Rebel battery, losing three or four prisoners and taking sixteen. General Lewis Wallace ordered out his division, and moved up from Crump's Landing a mile or two, and the troops stood under arms in the rain, that poured in torrents through the night, to be ready for an attack from that direction; but nothing came of it. There was more skirmishing on Saturday,—a continual firing along the picket lines. All supposed that the Rebels were making a reconnaissance. No one thought that one of the greatest battles of the war was close at hand. General Grant went down the river to Savannah on Saturday night. The troops dried their clothes in the sun, cooked their suppers, told their evening stories, and put out their lights at tattoo, as usual.

To get at the position of General Grant's army, let us start from Pittsburg Landing. It is a very busy place at the Landing. Forty or fifty steamboats are there, and hundreds of men are rolling out barrels of sugar, bacon, pork, beef, boxes of bread, bundles of hay, and thousands of sacks of corn. There are several hundred wagons waiting to transport the supplies to the troops. A long train winds up the hill towards the west.

Ascending the hill, you come to the forks of the roads. The right-hand road leads to Crump's Landing. You see General Smith's old division, which took the rifle-pits at Donelson, on the right-hand side of the road in the woods. It is commanded now by W. H. L. Wallace, who has been made a Brigadier-General for his heroism at Donelson. There have been many changes of commanders since that battle. Colonels who commanded regiments there are now brigade commanders.

Keeping along the Shiloh road a few rods, you come to the road which leads to Hamburg. Instead of turning up that, you keep on a little farther to the Ridge road, leading to Corinth. General Prentiss's division is on that road, two miles out, towards the southwest. Instead of taking that road, you still keep on the right-hand one, travelling nearly west all the while, and you come to McClernand's division, which is encamped in a long line on both sides of the road. Here you see Dresser's, Taylor's, Schwartz's, and McAllister's batteries, and all those regiments which fought so determinedly at Donelson. They face northwest. Their line is a little east of the church.

Passing over to the church, you see that a number of roads centre there,—one coming in from the northwest, which will take you to Purdy; one from the northeast, which will carry you to Crump's Landing; the road up which you have travelled from Pittsburg Landing; one from the southeast, which will take you to Hamburg; and one from the southwest, which is the lower road to Corinth.

You see, close by the church, on both sides of this lower road to Corinth, General Sherman's division, not facing northwest, but nearly south. McClernand's left and Sherman's left are close together. They form the two sides of a triangle, the angle being at the left wings. They are in a very bad position to be attacked.

Take the Hamburg road now, and go southeast two miles and you come to the crossing of the Ridge road to Corinth, where you will find General Prentiss's division, before mentioned. Keeping on, you come to Lick Creek. It has high, steep banks. It is fordable at this point, and Colonel Stuart's brigade of Sherman's division is there, guarding the crossing. The brook which gurgles past the church empties into the creek. You see that Prentiss's entire division, and the left wing of McClernand's, is between Stuart's brigade and the rest of Sherman's division. There are detached regiments encamped in the woods near the Landing, which have just arrived, and have not been brigaded. There are also two regiments of cavalry in rear of these lines. There are several pieces of siege artillery on the top of the hill near the Landing, but there are no artillerists or gunners to serve them.

You see that the army does not expect to be attacked. The cavalry ought to be out six or eight miles on picket; but they are here, the horses quietly eating their oats. The infantry pickets ought to be out three or four miles, but they are not a mile and a half advanced from the camp. The army is in a bad position to resist a sudden attack from a superior force. McClernand ought not to be at right angles with Sherman, Stuart ought not to be separated from his division by Prentiss, and General Lewis Wallace is too far away to render prompt assistance. Besides, General Grant is absent, and there is no commander-in-chief on the field. You wonder that no preparations have been make to resist an attack, no breastworks thrown up, no proper disposition of the forces, no extended reconnoissances by the cavalry, and that, after the skirmishing on Friday and Saturday, all hands should lie down so quietly in their tents on Saturday night. They did not dream that fifty thousand Rebels were ready to strike them at daybreak.

General Johnston's plan of attack was submitted to his corps commanders and approved by them. It was to hurl the entire army upon Prentiss and Sherman. He had four lines of troops, extending from Lick Creek on the right to the southern branch of Snake Creek on the left, a distance of about two miles and a half.

The front line was composed of Major-General Hardee's entire corps, with General Gladden's brigade of Bragg's corps added on the right. The artillery was placed in front, followed closely by the infantry. Squadrons of cavalry were thrown out on both wings to sweep the woods and drive in the Union pickets.

About five hundred yards in rear of Hardee was the second line, Bragg's corps in the same order as Hardee's. Eight hundred yards in rear of Bragg was General Polk, his left wing supported by cavalry, his batteries in position to advance at a moment's notice. The reserve, under General Breckenridge, followed close upon Polk. Breckenridge's and Polk's corps were both reckoned as reserves. They had instructions to act as they thought best. There were from ten to twelve thousand men in each line.

The Rebel troops had received five days' rations on Friday,—meat and bread in their haversacks. They were not permitted to kindle a fire except in holes in the ground. No loud talking was allowed; no drums beat the tattoo, no bugle-note rang through the forest. They rolled themselves in their blankets, knowing at daybreak they were to strike the terrible blow. They were confident of success. They were assured by their officers it would be an easy victory, and that on Sunday night they should sleep in the Yankee camp, eat Yankee bread, drink real coffee, and have new suits of clothes.

In the evening General Johnston called his corps commanders around his bivouac fire for a last talk before the battle. Although Johnston was commander-in-chief, Beauregard planned the battle. Johnston was Beauregard's senior, but the battle-ground was in Beauregard's department. He gave directions to the officers.

Mr. William G. Stevenson, of Kentucky, who was in Arkansas when the war broke out, was impressed into the Rebel service. He acted as special *aide-de-camp* to General Breckenridge in that battle. He escaped from the Rebel service a few months later, and has published an interesting narrative of what he saw.[8] He stood outside the circle of generals waiting by his horse in the darkness to carry any despatch for his commander. He gives this description of the scene:

> In an open space, with a dim fire in the midst, and a drum on which to write, you could see grouped around their 'Little Napoleon,' as Beauregard was sometimes fondly called, ten or twelve generals, the flickering light playing over their eager faces, while they listened to his plans, and made suggestions as to the conduct of the fight.
>
> Beauregard soon warmed with his subject, and, throwing off his cloak, to give free play to his arms, he walked about the group, gesticulating rapidly, and jerking out his sentences with a strong French accent. All listened attentively, and the dim light, just revealing their countenances, showed their different emotions of confidence or distrust of his plans.
>
> General Sidney Johnston stood apart from the rest, with his tall, straight form standing out like a spectre against the dim sky, and the illusion was fully sustained by the light-gray military cloak which he folded around him. His face was pale, but wore a determined expression, and at times he drew nearer the centre of the ring, and said a few words, which were listened to with great attention. It may be he had some foreboding of the fate he was to meet on the morrow, for he did not seem to take much part in the discussion.
>
> General Breckenridge lay stretched out on a blanket near the fire, and occasionally sat upright and added a few words of counsel. General Bragg spoke frequently, and with earnestness. General Polk sat on a camp-stool at the outside of the circle, and held his head between his hands, buried in thought. Others reclined or sat in various positions.
>
> For two hours the council lasted, and as it broke up, and the generals were ready to return to their respective commands, I heard General Beauregard say, raising his hand and pointing in the direction of the Federal camp, whose drums we could plainly hear, 'Gentlemen, we sleep in the enemy's camp to-morrow night.'

---

8: *Thirteen Months in the Rebel Service.*

The Confederate General, the same writer says, had minute information of General Grant's position and numbers. This knowledge was obtained through spies and informers, some of whom lived in the vicinity, had been in and out of Grant's camp again and again, and knew every foot of ground.

Under these circumstances, with a superior force, with accurate knowledge of the position of every brigade in General Grant's army, with troops in the best spirits, enthusiastic, ardent, expecting a victory, stealing upon a foe unsuspicious, unprepared, with brigades and divisions widely separated, with General Grant, the commander-in-chief, ten miles away, and General Buell's nearest troops twenty miles distant, the Rebel generals waited impatiently for the coming of the morning.

# CHAPTER 8

# The Battle
# From Daybreak Till Ten O'clock

It was a lovely morning. A few fleecy clouds floated in the sky. The trees were putting out their tender leaves. The air was fragrant with the first blossoms of spring. The birds were singing their sweetest songs.

At three o'clock the Rebel troops were under arms, their breakfasts eaten, their blankets folded, their knapsacks laid aside. They were to move unencumbered, that they might fight with more vigour. The morning brightened, and the long lines moved through the forest.

The Union army was asleep. The reveille had not been beaten. The soldiers were still dreaming of home, or awaiting the morning drumbeat. The mules and horses were tied to the wagons, whinnying for their oats and corn. A few teamsters were astir. Cooks were rekindling the smouldering camp-fires. The pickets, a mile out, had kept watch through the night. There had been but little firing. There was nothing to indicate the near approach of fifty thousand men. Beauregard had ordered that there should be no picket-firing through the night.

General Prentiss had strengthened his picket-guard on the Corinth Ridge road Saturday night. Some of his officers reported that Rebel cavalry were plenty in the woods. He therefore doubled his grand guard, and extended the line. He also ordered Colonel Moore, of the Twenty-first Missouri, to go to the front with five companies of his regiment. Colonel Moore marched at three o'clock. General Prentiss did not expect a battle, but the appearance of the Rebels along the lines led him to take these precautions.

About the time Colonel Moore reached the pickets the Rebel skirmishers came in sight. The firing began. The pickets resolutely maintained their ground, but the Rebels pushed on. Colonel Moore, hearing the firing, hastened forward. It was hardly light enough to distinguish men from trees, but the steady advance of the Rebels con-

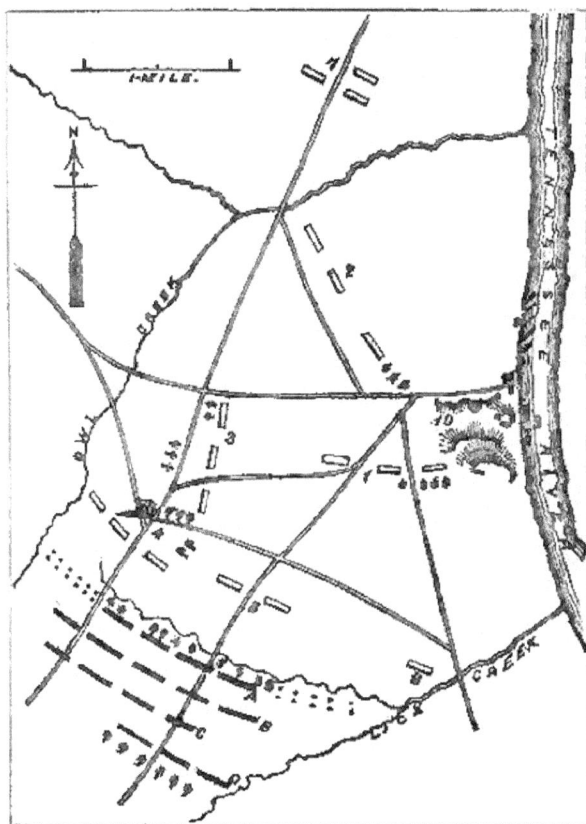

PITTSBURG LANDING.

| | |
|---|---|
| 1 Hurlburt's division. | 8 Gunboats. |
| 2 W. H. L. Wallace's division. | 9 Transports. |
| 3 McClernand's division. | 10 Ravine. |
| 4 Sherman's division. | A Hardee's line. |
| 5 Prentiss's division. | B Bragg's line. |
| 6 Stuart's brigade. | C Polk's line. |
| 7 Lewis Wallace's division. | D Breckenridge's reserves. |

vinced him that they were making a serious demonstration. He sent a messenger to General Prentiss for the balance of his regiment, which was sent forward. At the same time General Prentiss issued orders for the remainder of his division to form.

His entire force was seven regiments, divided into two brigades. The first brigade was commanded by Colonel Peabody, and contained the Twenty-fifth Missouri, Sixteenth Wisconsin, and Twelfth Michigan. The second brigade was composed of the Eighteenth and Twenty-third Missouri, Eighteenth Wisconsin, and Sixty-first Illinois. The

Twenty-third Missouri was at Pittsburg Landing, having just disembarked from a transport, and was not with the brigade till nearly ten o'clock. When the firing began, its commander, having been ordered to report to General Prentiss, moved promptly to join the division.

General Prentiss also sent an officer to Generals Hurlburt and Wallace, commanding the divisions in his rear, near the Landing, informing them that the Rebels were attacking his pickets in force. The firing increased. The Twenty-first Missouri gave a volley or two, but were obliged to fall back.

There had been a great deal of practising at target in the regiments, and every morning the pickets, on their return from the front, discharged their guns, and so accustomed had the soldiers become to the constant firing, that these volleys, so early in the morning, did not alarm the camp.

The orders which General Prentiss had issued were tardily acted upon. Many of the officers had not risen when the Twenty-first Missouri came back upon the double-quick, with Colonel Moore and several others wounded. They came in with wild cries. The Rebels were close upon their heels.

General Johnston had, as you have already seen, four lines of troops. The third corps was in front, commanded by Major-General Hardee, the second corps next, commanded by General Bragg; the first corps next, commanded by Major-General Polk, followed by the reserves under General Breckenridge.

General Hardee had three brigades, Hindman's, Cleburn's, and Wood's. General Bragg had two divisions, containing six brigades. The first division was commanded by General Ruggles, and contained Gibson's, Anderson's, and Pond's brigades. The second division was commanded by General Withers, and contained Gladden's, Chalmers's, and Jackson's brigades.

General Polk had two divisions, containing four brigades. The first division was commanded by General Clark, and contained Russell's and Stewart's brigades. The second division was commanded by Major-General Cheatham, and contained Johnson's and Stephens's brigades.

Breckenridge had Tabue's, Bowen's and Statham's brigades. General Gladden's brigade of Withers's division was placed on the right of Hardee's line. It was composed of the Twenty-first, Twenty-fifth, Twenty-sixth Alabama, and First Louisiana, with Robertson's battery. Hindman's brigade joined upon Gladden's. Gladden followed Colonel Moore's force, and fell upon Prentiss's camp.

Instantly there was a great commotion in the camp,—shouting, hallooing, running to and fro, saddling horses, seizing guns and cartridge-boxes, and forming in ranks. Gladden advanced rapidly, sending his bullets into the encampment. Men who had not yet risen were shot while lying in their tents.

But General Prentiss was all along his lines, issuing his orders, inspiring the men who, just awakened from sleep, were hardly in condition to act coolly. He ordered his whole force forward, with the exception of the Sixteenth Iowa, which had no ammunition, having arrived from Cairo on Saturday evening.

There was a wide gap between Prentiss's right and Sherman's left, and Hardee, finding no one to oppose him, pushed his own brigades into the gap, flanking Prentiss on one side and Sherman on the other, as you will see by a glance at the diagram.

Behind Gladden were Withers's remaining brigades, Chalmers's, and Jackson's. Chalmers was on the right, farther east than Gladden. He had the Fifth, Seventh, Ninth, Tenth Mississippi, and Fifty-second Tennessee, and Gage's battery.

Jackson had the Second Texas, Seventeenth, Eighteenth, and Nineteenth Alabama, and Girardey's battery. Chalmers moved rapidly upon Prentiss's left flank. Gage's and Robertson's batteries both opened with shell. Jackson came up on Prentiss's right, and in a short time his six regiments were engaged with twelve of Bragg's and two batteries.

They curled around Prentiss on both flanks, began to gain his rear to cut him off from the Landing, and separate him from Stuart's brigade of Sherman's division, which was a mile distant on the Hamburg road. The regiments on the left began to break, then those in the centre. The Rebels saw their advantage. Before them, dotting the hillside, were the much-coveted tents. They rushed on with a savage war-cry.

General Prentiss, aided by the cool and determined Colonel Peabody, rallied the faltering troops in front, but there was no power to stop the flood upon the flanks.

"Don't give way! Stand firm! Drive them back with the bayonet!" shouted Colonel Peabody, and some Missourians as brave as he remained in their places, loading and firing deliberately.

"On! on! forward boys!" cried General Gladden, leading his men; but a cannon-shot came screaming through the woods, knocked him from his horse, inflicting a mortal wound. The command devolved on Colonel Adams of the First Louisiana.

But the unchecked tide was flowing past Prentiss's gallant band.

Prentiss looked up to the right and saw it there, the long lines of men steadily moving through the forest. He galloped to the left and saw it there. The bayonets of the enemy were glistening between him and the brightening light in the east. His men were losing strength. They were falling before the galling fire, now given at short range. They were beginning to flee. He must fall back, and leave his camp, or be surrounded. His troops ran in wild disorder. Men, horses, baggage-wagons, ambulances, bounded over logs and stumps and through thickets in indescribable confusion. Colonel Peabody was shot from his horse, mortally wounded, and his troops, which had begun to show pluck and endurance, joined the fugitives.

Prentiss advised Hurlburt of the disaster. Hurlburt was prepared. He moved his division forward upon the double-quick. Prentiss's disorganized regiments drifted through it, but his ranks were unshaken.

The Rebels entered the tents of the captured camp, threw off their old clothes, and helped themselves to new garments, broke open trunks, rifled the knapsacks, and devoured the warm breakfast. They were jubilant; they shouted, danced, sung, and thought the victory won. Two or three hundred prisoners were taken, disarmed, and their pockets searched. They were obliged to give up all their money, and exchange clothes with their captors, and then were marched to the rear.

While this was taking place in Prentiss's division, Sherman's pickets were being driven back by the rapid advance of the Rebel lines. It was a little past sunrise when they came in, breathless, with startling accounts that the entire Rebel army was at their heels. The officers were not out of bed. The soldiers were just stirring, rubbing their eyes, putting on their boots, washing at the brook, or tending their camp-kettles. Their guns were in their tents; they had a small supply of ammunition. It was a complete surprise.

Officers jumped from their beds, tore open the tent-flies, and stood in undress to see what it was all about. The Rebel pickets rushed up within close musket range and fired.

"Fall in! Form a line! here, quick!" were the orders from the officers.

There was running in every direction. Soldiers for their guns, officers for their sabres, artillerists to their pieces, teamsters to their horses. There was hot haste, and a great hurly-burly.

General Hardee made a mistake at the outset. Instead of rushing up with a bayonet-charge upon Sherman's camp, and routing his unformed brigades in an instant, as he might have done, he unlimbered his batteries and opened fire.

The first infantry attack was upon Hildebrand's brigade, composed of the Fifty-third, Fifty-ninth, and Seventy-sixth Ohio, and the Fifty-third Illinois, which was on the left of the division. Next to it stood Buckland's brigade, composed of the Forty-eighth, Seventieth, and Seventy-second Ohio. On the extreme right, west of the church, was McDowell's brigade, composed of the Sixth Iowa, Fortieth Illinois, and Forty-sixth Ohio. Taylor's battery was parked around the church, and Waterhouse's battery was on a ridge a little east of the church, behind Hildebrand's brigade.

Notwithstanding this sudden onset, the ranks did not break. Some men ran, but the regiments formed with commendable firmness. The Rebel skirmishers came down to the bushes which border the brook south of the church, and began a scattering fire, which was returned by Sherman's pickets, which were still in line a few rods in front of the regiments. There was an open space between the Fifty-seventh and Fifty-third regiments of Hildebrand's brigade, and Waterhouse, under Sherman's direction, let fly his shells through the gap into the bushes. Taylor wheeled his guns into position on both sides of the church.

Hindman, Cleburn, and Wood advanced into the gap between Sherman and Prentiss, and swung towards the northwest upon Sherman's left flank. Ruggles, with his three brigades, and Hodgson's battery of Louisiana artillery, and Ketchum's battery, moved upon Sherman's front. He had Gibson's brigade on the right, composed of the Fourth, Thirteenth, and Nineteenth Louisiana, and the First Arkansas. Anderson's brigade was next in line, containing the Seventeenth and Twentieth Louisiana, and Ninth Texas, a Louisiana and a Florida battalion. Pond's brigade was on the left, and contained the Sixteenth and Eighteenth Louisiana, Thirty-eighth Tennessee, and two Louisiana battalions.

When the alarm was given, General Sherman was instantly on his horse. He sent a request to McClernand to support Hildebrand. He also sent word to Prentiss that the enemy were in front, but Prentiss had already made the discovery, and was contending with all his might against the avalanche rolling upon him from the ridge south of his position. He sent word to Hurlburt that a force was needed in the gap between the church and Prentiss. He was everywhere present, dashing along his lines, paying no attention to the constant fire aimed at him and his staff by the Rebel skirmishers, within short musket range. They saw him, knew that he was an officer of high rank, saw that he was bringing order out of confusion, and tried to pick him off. While galloping down to Hildebrand, his orderly, Halliday, was killed.

The fire from the bushes was galling, and Hildebrand ordered the Seventy-seventh and Fifty-seventh Ohio to drive out the Rebels. They advanced, and were about to make a charge, when they saw that they were confronted by Hardee's line, moving down the slope. The sun was just sending its morning rays through the forest, shining on the long line of bayonets. Instead of advancing, Hildebrand fell back and took position by Waterhouse, on the ridge. When Hildebrand advanced, two of Waterhouse's guns were sent across the brook, but they were speedily withdrawn, not too soon, however, for they were needed to crush Hindman and Cleburn who were crossing below Hildebrand.

Upon the south side of the brook there was a field and a crazy old farm-house. Ruggles came into the field, halted, and began to form for a rapid descent to the brook. His troops were in full view from the church.

"Pay your respects to those fellows over there," said Major Taylor to the officer commanding his own battery. Taylor was chief of artillery in Sherman's division, and was not in immediate command of his own battery. When he first saw them come into the field he thought they were not Rebels, but some of Prentiss's men, who had been out on the front. He hesitated to open fire till it was ascertained who they were. He rode down to Waterhouse, and told him to fire into the field. He galloped up to McDowell's brigade, where Barrett's battery was stationed, and told the officer commanding to do the same. In a moment the field was smoking hot, shells bursting in the air, crashing through Ruggles's ranks, and boring holes in the walls of the dilapidated old cabin. The Rebels could not face in the open field so severe a fire. Instead of advancing directly against the church, they moved into the woods east of the field, and became reinforcements to the brigades already well advanced into the gap between Sherman and Prentiss.

They came up on Hildebrand's left flank. The thick growth of hazel and alders along the brook concealed their movements. They advanced till they were not more than three hundred feet from the Fifty-third and Fifty-seventh Ohio before they began their fire. They yelled like demons, screeching and howling to frighten the handful of men supporting Waterhouse. Taylor saw that they intended an attack upon Waterhouse. He rode to the spot. "Give them grape and canister!" he shouted. It was done. The iron hail swept through the bushes. The yelling suddenly ceased. There were groans and moans instead. The advance in that direction was instantly checked.

But all the while the centre brigades of Hardee were pushing into the gap, and, without serious opposition, were gaining Sherman's left flank. Waterhouse began to limber up his guns for a retreat. Taylor feared a sudden panic.

"Contest every inch of ground. Keep cool. Give them grape. Let them have all they want," said Taylor.

Waterhouse unlimbered his guns again, wheeled them a little more to the east, almost northeast, and opened a fire which raked the long lines and again held them in check. Taylor sent to Schwartz, Dresser, and McAllister, connected with McClernand's division, to come into position and stop the flank movement.

This took time. The Rebels, seeing their advantages, and hoping to cut off Sherman, pushed on, and in five minutes were almost in rear of Waterhouse and Hildebrand. They gained the ridge which enfiladed Hildebrand. Cleburn and Wood swung up against Waterhouse. He wheeled still farther north, working his guns with great rapidity. They rushed upon him with the Indian war-whoop. His horses were shot. He tried to drag off his guns. He succeeded in saving three, but was obliged to leave the other three in their hands.

General McClernand had promptly responded to Sherman's request to support Hildebrand. Three regiments of Raitt's and Marsh's brigades were brought round into position in rear of Hildebrand. You remember that McClernand's division was facing northwest, and this movement, therefore, was a change of front to the southeast. The Eleventh Illinois formed upon the right of Waterhouse. The other two, the Forty-third and Thirtieth Illinois, were on the left, in rear. The fight was in Hildebrand's camp. There was a fierce contest. Two thirds of Hildebrand's men had been killed and wounded, or were missing. Most of the missing had fled towards the river. The regiments that remained were mixed up. The sudden onset had thrown them into confusion. There was but little order. Each man fought for himself. It was a brave little band, which tried to save the camp, but they were outnumbered and outflanked. The Eleventh Illinois lost six or eight of its officers by the first volley, yet they stood manfully against the superior force.

Meanwhile, Buckland and McDowell were in a hot fight against Anderson and Pond, who had moved to the western border of the field, and were forming against McDowell's right. Barrett and Taylor were thundering against them, but there were more cannon replying from the Rebel side. They were so far round on McDowell's flank, that the shells which flew over the heads of McDowell's men came past the church into Hildebrand's ranks. Sherman tried to hold his position by the church. He considered it to be of the utmost importance. He did not want to lose his camp. He exhibited great bravery. His horse was shot, and he mounted another. That also was killed, and he took a third, and, before night, lost his fourth. He encouraged his men, not only by his words, but by his reckless daring. Buckland's and McDowell's men recovered from the shock they first received. They became bull-dogs. Their blood was up. As often as the Rebels attempted to crowd McDowell back, they defeated the attempt. The two brigades with Taylor's and Barrett's batteries held their ground till after ten o'clock, and they would not have yielded then had it not been for disaster down the line.

Hildebrand rallied his men. About one hundred joined the Eleventh Illinois, of McClernand's division, and fought like tigers.

In the advance of Bragg's line, Gibson's brigade became separated from Anderson and Pond, Gibson moving to the right towards Prentiss, and they to the left towards Sherman. Several regiments of Polk's line immediately moved into the gap. It was a reinforcement of the centre, but it was also a movement which tended to disorganize the Rebel lines. Gibson became separated from his division commands, and the regiments from Polk's corps became disconnected from their brigades, but General Bragg directed them to join General Hindman.

They moved on towards McClernand, who was changing front and getting into position a half-mile in rear of Sherman. They were so far advanced towards Pittsburg Landing, that Sherman saw he was in danger of being cut off. He reluctantly gave the order to abandon his camp and take a new position. He ordered the batteries to fall back to the Purdy and Hamburg road. He saw Buckland and McDowell, and told them where to rally. Captain Behr had been posted on the Purdy road with his battery, and had had but little part in the fight. He was falling back, closely followed by Pond.

"Come into position out there on the right," said Sherman, pointing to the place where he wanted him to unlimber. There came a volley from the woods. A shot struck the Captain from his horse. The drivers and gunners became frightened, and rode off with the caissons, leaving five unspiked guns to fall into the hands of the Rebels! Sherman and Taylor, and other officers, by their coolness, bravery, and daring, saved Buckland and McDowell's brigades from a panic; and thus, after four hours of hard fighting, Sherman was obliged to leave his camp and fall back behind McClernand, who now was having a fierce fight with the brigades which had pushed in between Prentiss and Sherman.

The Rebels rejoiced over their success. Their loud hurrahs rose above the din of battle. They rushed into the tents and helped themselves to whatever they could lay their hands on, as had already been done in Prentiss's camps. Officers and men in the Rebel ranks alike forgot all discipline. They threw off their old gray rags, and appeared in blue uniforms. They broke open the trunks of the officers, and rifled the knapsacks of the soldiers. They seized the half-cooked breakfast, and ate like half-starved wolves. They found bottles of whiskey in some of the officers' quarters, and drank, danced, sung, hurrahed, and were half-crazy with the excitement of their victory.

Having taken this look at matters in the vicinity of the church, let us go towards the river, and see the other divisions.

It was about half past six o'clock in the morning when General Hurlburt received notice from General Sherman that the Rebels were driving in his pickets. A few minutes later he had word from Prentiss asking for assistance.

He sent Veatch's brigade, which you remember consisted of the Twenty-fifth Indiana, the Fourteenth, Fifteenth, and Forty-eighth Illinois, to Sherman. The troops sprang into ranks as soon as the order was issued, and were on the march in ten minutes.

Prentiss sent a second messenger, asking for immediate aid. Hurlburt in person led his other two brigades, Williams's and Lauman's. He had Mann's Ohio battery, commanded by Lieutenant Brotzman, Ross's battery, from Michigan, and Meyer's Thirteenth Ohio battery. He marched out on the Ridge road, and met Prentiss's troops, disorganized and broken, with doleful stories of the loss of everything. Prentiss and other officers were attempting to rally them.

Hurlburt formed in line of battle on the border of an old cotton-field on the Hamburg road. There were some sheds, and a log-hut with a great chimney built of mud and sticks, along the road. In front of the hut was a peach-orchard. Mann's battery was placed near the northeast corner of the field. Williams's brigade was placed on one side of the field, and Lauman's on the other, which made the line nearly a right angle. Ross's battery was posted on the right, and Meyer's on the left. This disposition of his force enabled Hurlburt to concentrate his fire upon the field and into the peach-orchard.

You see the position,—the long line of men in blue, in the edge of the woods, sheltered in part by the giant oaks. You see the log-huts, the mud chimney, the peach-trees in front, all aflame with pink blossoms. The field is as smooth as a house floor. Here and there are handfuls of cotton, the leavings of last year's crop. It is perhaps forty or fifty rods across the field to the forest upon the other side. Hurlburt and his officers are riding along the lines, cheering the men and giving directions. The fugitives from Prentiss are hastening towards the Landing. But a line of guards has been thrown out, and the men are rallying behind Hurlburt. The men standing in line along that field know that they are to fight a terrible battle. At first there is a little wavering, but they gain confidence, load their guns, and wait for the enemy.

Withers's division, which had pushed back Prentiss, moved upon Hurlburt's right. Gage's and Girardey's batteries opened fire. The first shot struck near Meyer's battery. The men never before had heard the shriek of a Rebel shell. It was so sudden, unexpected, and terrifying, that officers and men fled, leaving their cannon, caissons, horses, and everything. Hurlburt saw no more of them during the day. Indignant at the manifestation of cowardice, he rode down to Mann's battery, and called for volunteers to work the abandoned guns; ten men responded to the call. A few other volunteers were picked up, and although they knew but little of artillery practice, took their places beside the guns and opened fire. The horses with the caissons were dashing madly through the forest, increasing the confusion, but they were caught and brought in. You see that in battle men sometimes lose their presence of mind, and act foolishly. It is quite likely, however, that the troops fought all the more bravely for this display of cowardice. Many who were a little nervous, who had a strange feeling at the heart, did not like the exhibition, and resolved that they would not run.

At this time the fortunes of the Union army were dark. Prentiss had been routed. His command was a mere rabble. Hildebrand's brigade of Sherman's division was broken to pieces; there was not more than half a regiment left. The other two brigades of Sherman's division by the church were giving way. Half of Waterhouse's battery, and all but one of Behr's guns were taken. Sherman and Prentiss had been driven from their camps. Four of the six guns composing Meyer's battery could not be used for want of men. The three regiments which McClernand had sent to Sherman were badly cut to pieces. The entire front had been driven in. Johnston had gained a mile of ground. He had accomplished a great deal with little loss.

General Grant heard the firing at Savannah, ten miles down the river. It was so constant and heavy that he understood at once it was an attack. He sent a messenger post haste to General Buell, whose advance was ten miles east of Savannah, and then hastened to Pittsburg on a steamboat. He arrived on the ground about nine o'clock. Up to that hour there was no commander-in-chief, but each division commander gave such orders as he thought best. There was but little unity of action. Each commander was impressed with a sense of danger, and each was doing his best to hold the enemy in check.

The wide gap between Prentiss and Sherman, and the quick routing of Prentiss's regiments, enabled Hardee to push his middle brigades to the centre of the Union army without much opposition. Both of Hardee's flanks had been held back by the stout fight of Sherman on one side, the weaker resistance of Prentiss on the other. This gradually made the Rebel force into the form of a wedge, and at the moment when Hurlburt was waiting for their advance, the point of the wedge had penetrated beyond Hurlburt's right, but there it came against General W. H. L. Wallace's division.

When Hurlburt notified Wallace that Prentiss was attacked, that noble commander ordered his division under arms. You remember his position, near Snake Creek, and nearer the Pittsburg Landing than any other division. He at once moved in the direction of the firing, which brought him west of Hurlburt's position.

You remember that General McClernand had sent three regiments to General Sherman, and that they were obliged to change front. Having done that, he moved his other two brigades, the first under the command of Colonel Hare, including the Eighth and Eighteenth Illinois infantry and the Eleventh and Thirteenth Iowa, with Dresser's battery, and the third brigade with Schwartz's and McAllister's batteries. It was a complete change of front. These movements of Wallace and McClernand were directly against the two sides and the point of the wedge which Hardee was driving. Wallace marched southwest, and McClernand swung round facing southeast. They came up just in season to save Sherman from being cut off and also to save Veatch's brigade of Hurlburt's division from being overwhelmed.

McClernand's headquarters were in an old cotton-field. The camps of his regiments extended across the field and into the forest on both sides. He established his line on the south side of the field in the edge of the forest, determined to save his camp if possible. His men had seen hard fighting at Fort Donelson, and so had General Wallace's men. They were hardened to the scenes of battle, whereas

113

Sherman's, Prentiss's, and Hurlburt's men were having their first experience. Schwartz, McAllister, and Dresser had confronted the Rebels at Donelson, and so had Major Cavender with his eighteen pieces, commanded by Captains Stone, Richardson, and Walker.

This is a long and intricate story, and I fear you will not be able to understand it. The regiments at this hour were very much mixed up, and as the battle continued they became more so. Later in the day there was so much confusion that no correct account can ever be given of the positions of the regiments. Thousands of you, I doubt not, had friends in that battle, and you would like to know just where they stood. Let us therefore walk the entire length of the line while the Rebels are preparing for the second onset. Commencing on the extreme right, we find Sherman reforming with his left flank a little in rear of McClernand's right. There is McDowell's brigade on the right, the Sixth Iowa, Fourth Illinois, and Forty-sixth Ohio. Buckland's brigade next, the Forty-eighth, Seventieth, and Seventy-second Ohio. A few men of Hildebrand's brigade, not five hundred in all, of the Fifty-third, Fifty-seventh, and Seventy-sixth Ohio. Next the regiments of McClernand's division, the Eleventh Iowa, Eleventh, Twentieth, Forty-eighth, Forty-fifth, Seventeenth, Twenty-ninth, Forty-ninth, Forty-third, Eighth, and Eighteenth Illinois. Next Wallace's division, Seventh, Ninth, Twelfth, Fiftieth, and Fifty-second Illinois, the Twelfth, Thirteenth Iowa, and the Twenty-fifth, Fifty-second, and Fifty-sixth Indiana. I think that all of those regiments were there, although it is possible that one or two of them had not arrived. These are not all in the front line, but you see them in two lines. Some of them lying down behind the ridges waiting the time when they can spring up and confront the enemy.

Next in line you see Veatch's brigade of Hurlburt's division, the Twenty-fifth Indiana, the Fourteenth, Fifteenth, and Forty-sixth Illinois; then Williams's brigade, the Third Iowa, the Twenty-eighth, Thirty-second, and Forty-first Illinois, by the log-huts of the cotton-field on the Hamburg road. Here are Cavender's guns, eighteen of them. Next is Lauman's brigade,—not the one he commanded at Donelson in the victorious charge, but one composed of the Thirty-first and Forty-fourth Indiana, and the Seventeenth and Twenty-fifth Kentucky.

Behind Wallace and Hurlburt Prentiss is reforming his disorganized regiments, the Twenty-first, Twenty-third, and Twenty-fifth Missouri, Sixteenth and Eighteenth Wisconsin, and the Twelfth Michigan.

You remember that Stuart's brigade of Sherman's division was keeping watch on the Hamburg road at the Lick Creek crossing, towards the river from Prentiss. When Prentiss was attacked, he sent word to Stuart, who ordered his brigade under arms at once. He waited for orders. He saw after a while the Rebel bayonets gleaming through the woods between himself and Prentiss. He placed the Seventy-first Ohio on the right, the Fifty-fifth Illinois in the centre, and the Fifty-fourth on the left. These three regiments compose his brigade, and complete the list of those engaged in the fight on Sunday.

When the fight began in the morning, Stuart sent two companies across the creek to act as skirmishers, but before they could scale the high bluffs upon the south side, Statham's and Bowen's brigades, of Breckenridge's reserves, had possession of the ground, and they returned. Statham's batteries opened upon Stuart's camp. Breckenridge had moved round from his position in rear, and now formed the extreme right of Johnston. There were eight regiments and a battery in front of Stuart. The battery forced the Seventy-first Ohio from its position. It retired to the top of the ridge behind its camp-ground, which Stuart could have held against a superior force, had he not been outflanked. The Seventy-first, without orders, abandoned the position, retreated towards the Landing, and Stuart saw no more of them during the day.

He took a new position, with his two regiments, on the crest of the hill. East of him was a ravine. Breckenridge sent a body of cavalry and infantry across the creek to creep up this ravine, get in rear of Stuart's left flank, and with the masses hurrying past his right cut him off. Stuart determined to make a gallant resistance. He sent four companies of the Fifty-fourth Ohio, who took their position at the head of the ravine or gully which makes up from the creek towards the north. They crept into the thick bushes, hid behind the trees, and commenced a galling fire, forcing the cavalry back and stopping the advance of the infantry. The remainder of his force kept Statham back on the front. His line of fire was across an open field, and as often as Statham attempted to cross it, he was sent back by the well-directed volleys. Stuart received assurances from General McArthur, commanding one of Wallace's brigades, that he should be supported, but the supports could not be spared from the centre. Stuart maintained his position more than two hours, till his cartridge-boxes were emptied. When his ammunition failed, Statham and Bowen made another rush upon his left, and he saw that he must retreat or be taken prisoner. He fell back to Hurlburt's line, and formed the remnant of his brigade on the left, thus completing the line of battle which was established at ten o'clock.

Generals Bragg and Polk directed the attack on McClernand and Wallace. Pond's brigade was northwest of the church, Anderson's by the church, Cleburn's and Wood's east of it. Hindman's and the regiments of Polk's corps which had broken off from their brigades were in front of Wallace's right. These regiments belonged to Cheatham's division. The whole of his division was in front of Wallace.

Russell, Stewart, and Gibson were in front of Wallace's left. Gladden, Chalmers, and Jackson were on Hurlburt's right, while Breckenridge, having driven back Stuart, came up on his left.

The Rebels, confident of final victory, came up with great bravery, and commenced attacking McClernand, but they were confronted by men equally brave. Pond and Anderson charged upon the regiments on McClernand's right, but the charge was broken by the quick volleys of the Eleventh, Twentieth, and Forty-eighth Illinois. Cleburn and Wood rushed upon the Forty-fifth, Seventeenth, and Forty-ninth, which were in the centre of the division, but were repulsed. Then they swung against the Eleventh and Eighteenth, in front of McClernand's headquarters, but could not break the line. For a half-hour more, they stood and fired at long musket range. Dresser, McAllister, and Schwartz gave their batteries full play, but were answered by the batteries planted around the church, on the ground from which Sherman had been driven. Bragg advanced his men to short musket range, fifteen to twenty rods distant. Trees were broken off by the cannon-shot, splintered by the shells; branches were wrenched from the trunks, the hazel-twigs were cut by the storm of leaden hail. Many trees were struck fifty, sixty, and a hundred times. Officers and men fell on both sides very fast. Polk's brigades came up, and the united forces rushed upon the batteries. There was a desperate struggle. The horses were shot,—Schwartz lost sixteen, Dresser eighteen, and McAllister thirty. The guns were seized,—Schwartz lost three, McAllister two, and Dresser three. The infantry could not hold their ground. They fell back, took a new position, and made another effort to save their camp.

The woods rang with the hurrahs of the Rebels. The ground was thick with their dead and wounded, but they were winning. They had the largest army, and success stimulated them to make another attack. Bragg reformed his columns.

McClernand's second line of defence was near his camp. His men fought bravely to save it. Polk's brigades moved to the front, and charged upon the line, but they were checked. McClernand charged upon them, and in turn was repulsed. So the contest went on hour after hour.

Buckland and McDowell, of Sherman's command, were too much exhausted and disorganized by their long contest in the morning to take much part in this fight. They stood as reserves. Barrett and Taylor had used all their ammunition, and could not aid.

McClernand's right was unprotected. Bragg saw it, and moved round Anderson's, Pond's, and a portion of Stewart's brigades. There was a short struggle, and then the troops gave way. The men ran in confusion across the field swept by the Rebel artillery. The pursuers, with exultant cheers, followed, no longer in order, but each Rebel soldier running for the plunder in the tents. The contest was prolonged a little on the left, but the camp was in the hands of the Rebels, and McClernand and Sherman again fell back towards Wallace's camp.

Wallace was already engaged. The tide which had surged against Sherman and McClernand now came with increased force against his division. Beauregard aimed for the Landing, to seize the transports, using his force as a wedge to split the Union army off from the river. He might have deflected his force to Grant's right, and avoided what, as you will presently see, prevented him from accomplishing his object; but having been thus far successful in his plan, he continued the direct advance.

General Wallace was a very brave man. He was cool, had great presence of mind, and possessed the rare qualification of making his soldiers feel his presence. He could bring order out of confusion, and by a word, a look, or an act inspire his men. He posted Cavender's three batteries in commanding positions on a ridge, and kept his infantry well under cover behind the ridge. Cavender's men had fought under the brave General Lyon at Wilson's Creek in Missouri, and had been in half a dozen battles. The screaming of the shells was music to them.

From eleven till four o'clock the battle raged in front of Wallace. The men who had fought their first battle so determinedly at Donelson were not to be driven now.

Four times Hardee, Bragg, and Cheatham rushed upon Wallace's line, but were in each instance repulsed. Twice Wallace followed them as they retired after their ineffectual attempts to crush him, but he had not sufficient power to break their triple ranks. He could hold his ground, but he could not push the superior force. His coolness, endurance, bravery, stubbornness, his quick perception of all that was taking place, his power over his men, to make each man a hero, did much towards saving the army on that disastrous day.

General Bragg says: "Hindman's command was gallantly led to the attack, but recoiled under a murderous fire. The noble and gallant leader (Hindman) fell severely wounded. The command returned to its work, but was unequal to the heavy task. I brought up Gibson's brigade, and threw them forward to attack the same point. A very heavy fire soon opened, and after a short conflict this command fell back in considerable disorder. Rallying the different regiments by my staff officers and escort, they were twice more moved to the attack only to be driven back."[9]

In the morning, when the Rebels commenced the attack, you remember that Breckenridge, with the Rebel reserves, was in the rear; that he moved east, and came down towards the river in front of Stuart's brigade. General Johnston and staff were upon the hills which border the creek, examining the ground in front of Stuart and Hurlburt. Ross, Mann, and Walker were throwing shells across the creek.

General Breckenridge rode up to General Johnston and conversed with him.

"I will lead your men into the fight to-day, for I intend to show these Tennesseans and Kentuckians that I am no coward," said Johnston to Breckenridge.[10]

The people of the Southwest thought he was a coward, because he had abandoned Nashville without a fight.

Breckenridge brought up Statham's and Bowen's brigades against Hurlburt. He formed his line in the edge of the woods on the opposite side of the field. After an artillery fire of an hour, he moved into the centre of the field, rushed through the peach-orchard, and came close to Hurlburt's line by the log-cabin. But the field was fenced with fire. There was constant flashing from the muskets, with broad sheets of flame from the artillery. The Rebels were repulsed with shattered ranks.

Breckenridge sent his special aid to General Johnston for instructions.[11] As the aid rode up, a shell exploded above the General and his staff. A fragment cut through General Johnston's right thigh, severing an artery. He was taken from his horse, and died on the field at half past two o'clock.

---

9: Bragg's Report.
10: Stevenson.
11: Stevenson.

General Beauregard assumed command, and gave orders to keep General Johnston's death a secret, that the troops might not be discouraged.

Three times Breckenridge attempted to force Hurlburt back by attacking him in front, but as often as he advanced he was driven back. It was sad to see the wounded drag themselves back to the woods, to escape the storm, more terrible than the blast of the simoom, sweeping over the field. Hurlburt's regiments fired away all their ammunition, and Prentiss who had rallied his men, advanced to the front while the cartridge-boxes were refilled.

While this was doing, General Bragg gave up the command of his line in front of Wallace to another officer and rode down towards the river in front of Hurlburt and Prentiss. He says:

> There I found a strong force, consisting of three parts without a common head; being General Breckenridge with his reserve division pressing the enemy; Brigadier-General Withers with his division utterly exhausted, and taking a temporary rest; and Major-General Cheatham's division of Major-General Polk's command to their left and rear. The troops were soon put in motion again, responding with great alacrity to the command, 'Forward!'[12]

Just at this moment General Wallace, on the right, was mortally wounded. It was like taking away half the strength of his division. The men lost heart in a moment. The power which had inspired them was gone. The brave man was carried to the rear, followed by his division. The giving way of this division, and the falling back of Prentiss before the masses flanking the extreme left, was most disastrous. Prentiss was surrounded and taken prisoner with the remnant of his division, and Hurlburt's camp fell into the hands of the Rebels. Of this movement General Bragg says:

> The enemy were driven headlong from every position, and thrown in confused masses upon the river-bank, behind his heavy artillery and under cover of his gunboats at the Landing. He had left nearly all his light artillery in our hands, and some three thousand or more prisoners, who were cut off from their retreat by the closing in of our troops on the left under Major-General Polk, with a portion of his reserve corps, and Brigadier-General Ruggles, with Anderson's and Pond's brigades of his division.[13]

12: Bragg's Report.
13: Bragg's Report.

The woods rang with the exultant shouts of the Rebels, as Prentiss and his men were marched towards Corinth. They had possession of the camps of all the divisions except Wallace's. Beauregard had redeemed his promise. They could sleep in the enemy's camps.

## SUNDAY EVENING

Look at the situation of General Grant's army. It is crowded back almost to the Landing. It is not more than a mile from the river to the extreme right, where Sherman and McClernand are trying to rally their disorganized divisions. All is confusion. Half of the artillery is lost. Many of the guns remaining are disabled. Some that are good are deserted by the artillerymen. There is a stream of fugitives to the Landing, who are thinking only how to escape. There are thousands on the river-bank, crowding upon the transports. They have woeful stories. Instead of being in their places, and standing their ground like men, they have deserted their brave comrades, and left them to be overwhelmed by the superior force of the enemy.

As you look at the position of the army and the condition of the troops at this hour, just before sunset, there is not much to hope for. But there are some men who have not lost heart. "We shall hold them yet," says General Grant.

An officer with gold-lace bands upon his coat-sleeve, and a gold band on his cap, walks up-hill from the Landing. It is an officer of the gunboat *Tyler*, commanded by Captain Gwin, who thinks he can be of some service. Shot and shells from the Rebel batteries have been falling in the river, and he would like to toss some into the woods.

"Tell Captain Gwin to use his own discretion and judgment," is the reply.

The officer hastens back to the *Tyler*. The *Lexington* is by her side. The men spring to the guns, and the shells go tearing up the ravine, exploding in the Rebel ranks, now massed for the last grand assault. All day long the men of the gunboats have heard the roar of the conflict coming nearer and nearer, and have had no opportunity to take a part, but now their time has come. The vessels sit gracefully upon the placid river. They cover themselves with white clouds, and the deep-mouthed cannon bellow their loudest thunders, which roll miles away along the winding stream. It is sweet music to those disheartened men forming to resist the last advance of the Rebels, now almost within reach of the coveted prize.

Colonel Webster, General Grant's chief of staff, an engineer and artillerist, with a quick eye, has selected a line of defence. There is a deep ravine just above Pittsburg Landing, which extends north-west half a mile. There are five heavy siege-guns, three thirty-two-pounders, and two eight-inch howitzers on the top of the bluff by the Landing. They have been standing there a week, but there are no artillerists to man them. Volunteers are called for. Dr. Cornyn, Surgeon of the First Missouri Artillery, offers his services. Artillerists who have lost their guns are collected. Round shot and shell are carried up from the boats. Fugitives who have lost their regiments are put to work. Pork-barrels are rolled up and placed in a line. Men go to work with spades, and throw up a rude embankment. The heavy guns are wheeled into position to sweep the ravine and all the ground beyond. Everything is done quickly. There is no time for delay. Men work as never before. Unless they can check the enemy, all is lost. Energy, activity, determination, endurance, and bravery must be concentrated into this last effort.

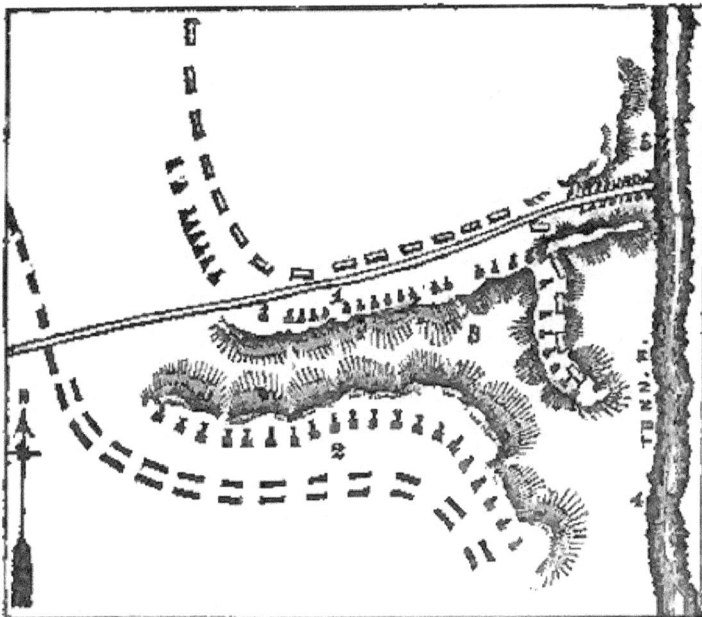

THE FIGHT AT THE RAVINE.

1 Union batteries.                    4 Gunboats.
2 Rebel batteries.                    5 Transports
3 Ravine.

Commencing nearest the river, on the ridge of the ravine, you see two of McAllister's twenty-four-pounders, next four of Captain Stone's ten pounders, then Captain Walker with one twenty-pounder, then Captain Silversparre with four twenty-pounder Parrott guns, which throw rifled projectiles, then two twenty-pound howitzers, which throw grape and canister. Then you come to the road which leads up to Shiloh church. There you see six brass field-pieces; then Captain Richardson's battery of four twenty-pounder Parrott guns; then a six-pounder and two twelve-pound howitzers of Captain Powell's battery; then the siege-guns, under Surgeon Cornyn and Captain Madison; then two ten-pounders, under Lieutenant Edwards, and two more under Lieutenant Timony. There are more guns beyond,— Taylor's, Willard's, and what is left of Schwartz's battery, and Mann's, Dresser's, and Ross's,—about sixty guns in all. The broken regiments are standing or lying down. The line, instead of being four miles long, as it was in the morning, is not more than a mile in length now. The regiments are all mixed up. There are men from a dozen in one, but they can fight notwithstanding that.

The Rebel commanders concentrate all their forces near the river, to charge through the ravine, scale the other side, rush down the road and capture the steamboats. They plant their batteries along the bank, bringing up all their guns, to cut their way by shot and shell. If they can but gain a foothold on the other side, the day is theirs. The Union army will be annihilated, Tennessee redeemed. Buell will be captured or pushed back to the Ohio River. The failing fortunes of the Confederacy will revive. Recognition by foreign nations will be secured. How momentous the hour!

Beauregard's troops were badly cut to pieces, and very much disorganized. The Second Texas, which had advanced through the peach-orchard, was all gone, and was not reorganized during the fight. Colonel Moore, commanding a brigade, says:

So unexpected was the shock, that the whole line gave way from right to left in utter confusion. The regiments became so scattered and mixed that all efforts to reform them became fruitless.[14]

Chalmers's brigade was on the extreme right. What was left of Jackson's came next. Breckenridge, with his shattered brigades, was behind Chalmers. Trabue, commanding a brigade of Kentuckians, was comparatively fresh. Withers's, Cheatham's, and Ruggles's divi-

---

14: Colonel Moore's Report.

sions were at the head of the ravine. Gibson, who had been almost annihilated, was there. Stewart, Anderson, Stephens, and Pond were on the ground from which Wallace had been driven. As the brigades filed past Beauregard, he said to them, "Forward, boys, and drive them into the Tennessee."[15]

The Rebel cannon open. A sulphurous cloud borders the bank. The wild uproar begins again. Opposite, another cloud rolls upward. There are weird shriekings across the chasm, fierce howlings from things unseen. Great oaks are torn asunder, broken, shattered, splintered. Cannon are overturned by invisible bolts. There are explosions in the earth and in the air. Men, horses, wagons, are lifted up, thrown down, torn to pieces, dashed against the trees. Commands are cut short; for while the words are on the lips the tongue ceases to articulate, the muscles relax, and the heart stops its beating,—all the springs of life broken in an instant.

Wilder, deeper, louder the uproar. Great shells from the gunboats fly up the ravine. The gunners aim at the cloud along the southern bank. They rake the Rebel lines, while the artillery massed in front cuts them through and through.

Bragg orders an advance. The brigades enter the ravine, sheltered in front by the tall trees above and the tangled undergrowth beneath. They push towards the northern slope.

"Grape and canister now!"

"Give them double charges!"

"Lower your guns!"

"Quick! Fire!"

The words run along the line. Moments are ages now. Seconds are years. How fast men live when everything is at stake! Ah! but how fast they die down in that ravine! Up, down, across, through, over it, drive the withering blasts, cutting, tearing, sweeping through the column, which shakes, wavers, totters, crumbles, disappears.

General Chalmers says:

We received orders from General Bragg to drive the enemy into the river. My brigade, together with General Jackson's brigade, filed to the right, formed facing the river, and endeavoured to press forward to the water's edge; but in attempting to mount the last ridge, we were met by a fire from a whole line of batteries, protected by infantry and assisted by shells from the

15: Ruggles's Report.

gunboats. Our men struggled vainly to ascend the hill, which was very steep, making charge after charge without success; but continued the fight till night closed hostilities.[16]

Says Colonel Fagan, of the First Arkansas, of Gibson's brigade:

Three different times did we go into that 'Valley of Death,' and as often were forced back by overwhelming numbers, entrenched in a strong position. That all was done that could possibly be done, the heaps of killed and wounded left there give ample evidence.[17]

Colonel Allen, of the Fourth Louisiana, says:

A murderous fire was poured into us from the masked batteries of grape and canister, and also from the rifle-pits. The regiment retired, formed again, and again charged. There fell many of my bravest and best men, in the thick brushwood, without ever seeing the enemy.[18]

It is sunset. The day has gone. It has been a wild, fierce, disastrous conflict. Beauregard has pushed steadily on towards the Landing. He is within musket-shot of the steamers, of the prize he so much covets. He has possession of all but one of the division camps. He can keep his promise made to his soldiers; they can sleep in the camps of the Union army. This is his first serious check. He has lost many men. His commander-in-chief is killed, but he is confident he can finish in the morning the work which has gone on so auspiciously, for Buell has not arrived.

He has done a good day's work. His men have fought well, but they are exhausted. Tomorrow morning he will finish General Grant. Thus he reasons.[19]

General Grant was right in his calculations. The Rebels have been checked at last. At sunset they who stand upon the hill by the Landing discover on the opposite bank men running up the road, panting for breath. Above them waves the Stars and Stripes. There is a buzz, a commotion, among the thousands by the river-side.

"It is Buell's advance!"

"Hurrah! hurrah! hurrah!"

16: Chalmers's Report.
17: Colonel Fagan's Report.
18: Colonel Allen's Report.
19: Beauregard's Report.

The shouts ring through the forest. The wounded lift their weary heads, behold the advancing line, and weep tears of joy. The steamers cast off their fastenings. The great wheels plash the gurgling water. They move to the other side. The panting soldiers of the army of the Ohio rush on board. The steamer settles to the guards with her precious cargo of human life; re-crosses the river in safety. The line of blue winds up the bank. It is Nelson's division. McCook's and Crittenden's divisions are at Savannah. Lewis Wallace's division from Crump's Landing is filing in upon the right, in front of Sherman and McClernand. There will be four fresh divisions on Monday morning. The army is safe. Buell will not be pushed back to the Ohio. Recognition will not come from France and England in consequence of the great Rebel victory at Shiloh.

Through the night the shells from the gunboats crashed along the Rebel lines. So destructive was the fire, that Beauregard was obliged to fall back from the position he had won by such a sacrifice of life. There was activity at the Landing. The steamers went to Savannah, took on board McCook's and Crittenden's divisions of Buell's army, and transported them to Pittsburg. Few words were spoken as they marched up the hill in the darkness, with the thousands of wounded on either hand, but there were many silent thanksgivings that they had come. The wearied soldiers lay down in battle line to broken sleep, with their loaded guns beside them. The sentinels stood, like statues, in silence on the borders of that valley of death, watching and waiting for the morning.

The battle-cloud hung like a pall above the forest. The gloom and darkness deepened. The stars, which had looked calmly down from the depths of heaven, withdrew from the scene. A horrible scene! for the exploding shells had set the forest on fire. The flames consumed the withered leaves and twigs of the thickets, and crept up to the helpless wounded, to friend and foe alike. There was no hand but God's to save them. He heard their cries and groans. The rain came, extinguishing the flames. It drenched the men in arms, waiting for daybreak to come to renew the strife, but there were hundreds of wounded, parched with fever, restless with pain, who thanked God for the rain.

## MONDAY

Beauregard laid his plans to begin the attack at daybreak. Grant and Buell resolved to do the same,—not to stand upon the defensive, but to astonish Beauregard by advancing. Nelson's division was placed on the left, nearest the river, Crittenden's next, McCook's beyond, and Lewis

Wallace on the extreme right,—all fresh troops,—with Grant's other divisions, which had made such a stubborn resistance, in reserve.

In General Nelson's division, you see nearest the river Colonel Ammen's brigade, consisting of the Thirty-sixth Indiana, Sixth and Twenty-fourth Ohio; next, Colonel Bruer's brigade, First, Second, and Twentieth Kentucky; next, Colonel Hazen's brigade, Ninth Indiana, Sixth Kentucky, and Forty-first Ohio. Colonel Ammen's brigade arrived in season to take part in the contest at the ravine on Sunday evening.

General Crittenden's division had two brigades: General Boyle's and Colonel W. L. Smith's. General Boyle had the Nineteenth and Fifty-ninth Ohio, and Ninth and Thirteenth Kentucky. Colonel Smith's was composed of the Thirteenth Ohio, and Eleventh and Twenty-sixth Kentucky, with Mendenhall's battery, belonging to the United States Regular Army, and Bartlett's Ohio battery.

General McCook's division had three brigades. The first was commanded by General Rousseau, consisting of the First Ohio, Sixth Indiana, Third Kentucky, and battalions of the Fifteenth, Sixteenth, and Nineteenth Regular Infantry. The second brigade was commanded by Brigadier-General Gibson, and consisted of the Thirty-second and Thirty-ninth Indiana, and Forty-ninth Ohio. The third brigade was commanded by Colonel Kirk, and consisted of the Thirty-fourth Illinois, Twenty-ninth and Thirtieth Indiana, and Seventy-seventh Pennsylvania.

General Lewis Wallace's division, which had been reorganized after the battle of Fort Donelson, now consisted of three brigades. The first was commanded by Colonel Morgan L. Smith, and consisted of the Eighth Missouri, Eleventh and Twenty-fourth Indiana, and Thurber's Missouri battery. The second brigade was commanded by Colonel Thayer, and contained the same regiments that checked the Rebels at the brook west of Fort Donelson,—the First Nebraska, Twenty-third and Sixty-eighth Ohio, with Thompson's Indiana battery. The third brigade was commanded by Colonel Whittlesey, and was composed of the Twentieth, Fifty-sixth, Seventy-sixth, and Seventy-eighth Ohio.

Two brigades of General Wood's division arrived during the day, but not in season to take part in the battle.

Beauregard's brigades were scattered during the night. They had retired in confusion before the terrible fire at the ravine from the gunboats. Officers were hunting for their troops, and soldiers were searching for their regiments, through the night. The work of reorganizing was going on when the pickets at daylight were driven in by the advance of the Union line.

Beauregard, Bragg, Hardee, and Polk all slept near the church. There was no regularity of divisions, brigades, or regiments. Ruggles was west of the church with two of his brigades. Trabue's brigade of Breckenridge's reserves was there. Breckenridge, with his other brigades, or what was left of them, was east of the church, also the shattered fragments of Withers's division. Gladden's brigade had crumbled to pieces, and Colonel Deas, commanding it, was obliged to pick up stragglers of all regiments. Russell and Stewart were near Prentiss's camp. Cheatham was in the vicinity, but his regiments were dwindled to companies, and scattered over all the ground.

Beauregard had established a strong rear-guard, and had issued orders to shoot all stragglers. The order was rigidly enforced, and the runaways were brought back and placed in line. Although exhausted, disorganized, and checked, the Rebels had not lost heart. They were confident of victory, and at once rallied when they found the Union army was advancing.

Look once more at the position of the divisions. Nelson is on the ground over which Stuart and Hurlburt retreated. Crittenden is where Prentiss was captured, McCook where McClernand made his desperate stand, and Lewis Wallace where Sherman's line gave way.

The gunboats, by their constant fire during the night, had compelled the Rebels to fall back in front of Nelson. It was a little after five o'clock when Nelson threw forward his skirmishers, and advanced his line. He came upon the Rebels half-way out to Lick Creek, near the peach-orchard. The fight commenced furiously. Beauregard was marching brigades from his left, and placing them in position for a concentrated attack to gain the Landing. General Crittenden had not advanced, and Nelson was assailed by a superior force. He held his ground an hour, but he had no battery. He had been compelled to leave it at Savannah. He sent an aid to General Buell requesting artillery. Mendenhall was sent. He arrived just in time to save the brigade from an overwhelming onset. The Rebels were advancing when he unlimbered his guns, but his quick discharges of grape at short range threw them into confusion.

It astonished General Beauregard. He had not expected it. He was to attack and annihilate Grant, not be attacked and driven.[20] He ordered up fresh troops from his reserves, and the contest raged with increased fury.

Nelson, seeing the effect of Mendenhall's fire, threw Hazen's bri-

---

20: Beauregard's Report.

gade forward. It came upon the battery which had been cutting them to pieces. With a cheer they sprang upon the guns, seized them, commenced turning them upon the fleeing enemy. The Rebel line rallied and came back, followed by fresh troops. There was a short, severe struggle, and Hazen was forced to leave the pieces and fall back. Then the thunders rolled again. The woods were sheets of flame.[21] The Rebels brought up more of their reserves, and forced Nelson to yield his position. He fell back a short distance, and again came into position. He was a stubborn man,—a Kentuckian, a sailor, who had been round the world. His discipline was severe. His men had been well drilled, and were as stubborn as their leader.

"Send me another battery, quick!" was his request, made to General Buell.

Tirrell's battery, which had just landed from a steamer, went up the hill, through the woods, over stumps and trees, the horses leaping as if they had caught the enthusiasm of the commander of the battery. Captain Tirrell had a quick eye.

"Into position there. Lively, men! Caissons to the rear!" were his words of command. The gunners sprang from the carriages to the ground. The caissons wheeled, bringing the heads of the horses towards the Landing, trotted off eight or ten rods and took position sheltered by a ridge of land. Captain Tirrell rode from gun to gun.

"Fire with shell, two-second fuses," he said to the lieutenants commanding his two ten-pounder Parrott guns.

"Grape and canister," he said to the officers commanding the four brass twelve-pounders. Its fire was terrific. Wherever his guns were turned there was silence along the Rebel lines. Their musketry ceased. Their columns staggered back. All the while Mendenhall was pounding them. The Nineteenth Ohio, from Crittenden's division, came down upon the run, joined the brigade, and the contest went on again. The Rebels, instead of advancing, began to lose the ground they had already won.

Crittenden and McCook advanced a little later. They came upon the enemy, which had quiet possession of McClernand's and Sherman's camps. Beauregard's headquarters were there. The Rebels, finding themselves assailed, made a desperate effort to drive back the advancing columns. Rousseau advanced across the open field, over the ground so hotly contested by McClernand the day before. This movement made a gap between McCook and Crittenden. Beauregard saw

21: Nelson's Report.

it, threw Cheatham and Withers into the open space. They swung round square against Rousseau's left, pouring in a volley which staggered the advancing regiments. The Thirty-second Indiana regiment, Colonel Willich commanding, was on the extreme right of McCook's division. They had been in battle before, and were ordered across to meet the enemy. You see them fly through the woods in rear of Rousseau's brigade. They are upon the run. They halt, dress their ranks as if upon parade, and charge upon the Rebels. Colonel Stambough's Seventy-seventh Pennsylvania follows. Then all of Kirk's brigade. It is a change of position and a change of front, admirably executed, just at the right time, for Rousseau is out of ammunition, and is obliged to fall back. McCook's third brigade, General Gibson, comes up. Rousseau is ready again, and at eleven o'clock you see every available man of that division contending for the ground around the church. Meanwhile Wallace is moving over the ground on the extreme right, where Sherman fought so bravely. Sherman, Hurlburt, and the shattered regiments of W. H. L. Wallace's division, now commanded by McArthur, follow in reserve. Driven back by Nelson, the Rebel forces concentrate once more around the church for a final struggle. Wallace watches his opportunities. He gains a ridge. His men drop upon the ground, deliver volley after volley, rise, rush nearer to the enemy, drop once more, while the grape and canister sweep over them. Thus they come to close quarters, and then regiment after regiment rises, and delivers its fire. It is like the broadsides of a man-of-war.

The time had come for a general advance. Nelson, Crittenden, McCook, Wallace, almost simultaneously charged upon the enemy. It was too powerful to be resisted. The Rebels gave way, retreated from the camps which they had occupied a single night, fled past the church, across the brook, up through the old cotton-field on the south side, to the shelter of the forest on the top of the ridge beyond. The battle was lost to them. Exultant cheers rang through the forest for the victory won.

If I were to go through all the details, as I might, and write how Crittenden's brigades pressed on, and captured Rebel batteries; how the Rebels tried to overwhelm him; how the tide of battle surged from hill to hill; how the Rebels tried to cut McCook to pieces; how Wallace's division flanked the enemy at Owl Creek; how Rousseau's brigade fought in front of McClernand's camp; how the Fifth Kentucky charged upon a battery, and captured two guns which were cutting them up with grape and canister, and four more which were disabled and could not be dragged off by the enemy; how Colonel Willich, commanding the Thirty-second Indiana, finding some of his men were getting excited, stopped firing, and drilled them, ordering, presenting, and supporting arms, with the balls whistling through his ranks; how the men became cool and steady, and went in upon a charge at last with a wild hurrah, and a plunge of the bayonet that forced the Rebels to give up McClernand's camp; how Colonel Ammen coolly husked ears of corn for his horse, while watching the fight, with the shells falling all around him; how Colonel Kirk seized a flag and bore it in advance of his brigade; how Colour-Sergeant William Ferguson of the Thirteenth Missouri was shot down, how Sergeant Beem of Company C seized the flag before it touched the ground, and advanced it still farther; how Beauregard was riding madly along the lines by the church, trying to rally his men, when Thurber's battery opened, and broke them up again; how, at noon, he saw it was no use; how he drew off his men, burned his own camp, and went back to Corinth, defeated, his troops disheartened, leaving his killed and hundreds of his wounded on the field; how the Union army recovered all the cannon lost on Sunday;—if I were to write it all out, I should have no room to tell you what Commodore Foote was doing all this time on the Mississippi.

It was a terrible fight. The loss on each side was nearly equal,—about thirteen thousand killed, wounded, and missing, or twenty-six thousand in all.

I had a friend killed in the fight on Sunday,—Captain Carson, commanding General Grant's scouts. He was tall and slim, and had sparkling black eyes. He had travelled all over Missouri, Kentucky, and Tennessee, had often been in the Rebel camps. He was brave, almost fearless, and very adroit. He said to a friend, when the battle began in the morning, that he should not live through the day. But he was very active, riding recklessly through showers of bullets. It was just at sunset when he rode up to General Grant with a despatch from General Buell. He dismounted, and sat down upon a log to rest, but the next moment his head was carried away by a cannon-ball. He performed his duties faithfully, and gave his life willingly to his country.

You have seen how the army was surprised, how desperately it fought, how the battle was almost lost, how the gunboats beat back the exultant Rebels, how the victory was won. Beauregard was completely defeated; but he telegraphed to Jefferson Davis that he had won a great victory. This is what he telegraphed—

Corinth
April 8th, 1862
To the Secretary of War
Richmond
We have gained a great and glorious victory. Eight to ten thousand prisoners and thirty-six pieces of cannon. Buell reinforced Grant, and we retired to our entrenchments at Corinth, which we can hold. Loss heavy on both sides.

*Beauregard*

You see that, having forsworn himself to his country, he did not hesitate to send a false despatch, to mislead the Southern people and cover up his mortifying defeat.

The Rebel newspapers believed Beauregard's report. One began its account thus:

*Glory! glory! glory! victory! victory!* I write from Yankee papers. Of all the victories that have ever been on record, ours is the most complete. Bull Run was nothing in comparison to our victory at Shiloh. General Buell is killed, General Grant wounded and taken prisoner. Soon we will prove too much for them, and they will be compelled to let us alone. Our brave boys have driven them to the river, and compelled them to flee to their gunboats. The day is ours.[22]

The people of the South believed all this; but when the truth was known their hopes went down lower than ever, for they saw it was a disastrous defeat.

On the Sabbath after the battle, the chaplains of the regiments had religious exercises. How different the scene! Instead of the cannonade, there were prayers to God. Instead of the musketry, there were songs of praise. There were tears shed for those who had fallen, but there were devout thanksgivings that they had given their lives so freely for their country and for the victory they had achieved by their sacrifice.

One of the chaplains, in conducting the service, read a hymn, commencing:
*Look down, O Lord, O Lord forgive;*
*Let a repenting rebel live.*

But he was suddenly interrupted by a patriotic soldier, who cried, "No sir, not unless they lay down their arms, every one of them."

---

22: Captain Geer.

He thought the chaplain had reference to the Rebels who had been defeated.

After the battle, a great many men and women visited the ground, searching for the bodies of friends who had fallen. Lieutenant Pfieff, an officer of an Illinois regiment, was killed, and his wife came to obtain his body. No one knew where he was buried. The poor woman wandered through the forest, examining all the graves. Suddenly a dog, poor and emaciated, bounded towards her, his eyes sparkling with pleasure, and barking his joy to see his mistress. When her husband went to the army, the dog followed him, and was with him through the battle, watched over his dead body through the terrible contest, and after he was buried, remained day and night a mourner! He led his mistress to the spot. The body was disinterred. The two sorrowful ones, the devoted wife and the faithful brute, watched beside the precious dust till it was laid in its final resting-place beneath the prairie-flowers.

CHAPTER 9

# Evacuation of Columbus

The Rebels, at the beginning of the war fortified Columbus, in Kentucky, which is twenty miles below Cairo on the Mississippi River. There the bluffs are very high, and are washed at their base by the mighty stream. Cannon placed on the summit have long range. A great deal of labour was expended to make it an impregnable place. There were batteries close down to the water under the hill, with heavy guns. A gallery was cut along the side of the bluff, a winding, zigzag passage, which, with many crooks and turns, led to the top of the hill. They had numerous guns in position on the top, to send shot and shell down upon Commodore Foote, should he attempt to descend the river. They built a long line of earthworks to protect the rear, entrenchments and stockades,—which are strong posts set in the ground, making a close fence, with holes here and there through which the riflemen and sharpshooters could fire.

They cut down the trees and made *abatis*. There were several lines of defence. They stretched a great iron chain across the river, supporting it by barges which were anchored in the stream. They gave out word that the river was effectually closed against commerce till the independence of the Confederacy was recognized.

When the war commenced, there was a man named Maury, a lieutenant in the United States service, and who was connected with the National Observatory in Washington. He was thought to be a scientific, practical man. He had been educated by the government, had received great pay, and was in a high position; but he forgot all that, and joined the Rebels. He imitated General Floyd, and stole public property, carrying off from the National Observatory valuable scientific papers which did not belong to him. He was employed by the Rebel government to construct torpedoes and infernal machines for

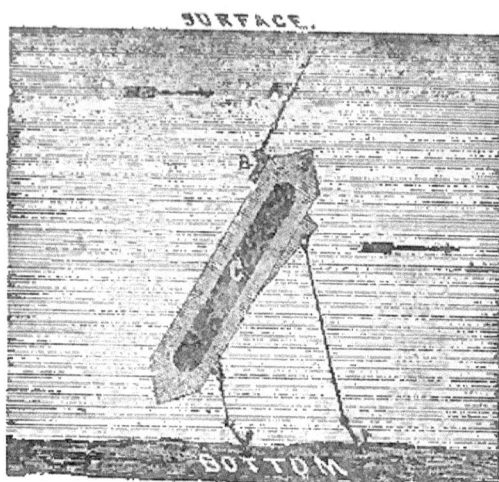

A REBEL TORPEDO.

blowing up Commodore Foote's gunboats. He had several thousand made,—some for the land, which were planted around Columbus in rear of the town, and which were connected with a galvanic battery by a telegraph wire, to be exploded at the right moment, by which he hoped to destroy thousands of the Union troops. He sunk several hundred in the river opposite Columbus. They were oblong cylinders of wrought iron, four or five feet in length; inside were two or three hundred pounds of powder. Two small anchors held the cylinder in its proper place. It was air tight, and therefore floated in the water. At the upper end there was a projecting iron rod, which was connected with a percussion gun-lock. If anything struck the rod with much force, it would trip the lock, and explode the powder. At least, Mr. Maury thought so. The above engraving will show the construction of the torpedoes, and how they were placed in the water. The letter A represents the iron rod reaching up almost to the surface of the water. At B it is connected with the lock, which is inside the cylinder, and not represented. C represents the powder. The arrows show the direction of the current.

One day he tried an experiment. He sunk a torpedo, and let loose a flat-boat, which came down with the current and struck the iron rod. The powder exploded and sent the flat high into the air. Thousands of Rebel soldiers stood on the bluffs and saw it. They hurrahed and swung their hats. Mr. Maury was so well pleased that the river was planted with them, above, in front, and below the town. He thought that Commodore Foote and all his gunboats would be blown out of the water if they attempted to descend the stream.

But the workmanship was rude. The parts were not put together with much skill. Mr. Maury showed that his science was not practical. He forgot that the river was constantly rising and falling, that sometimes the water would be so high the gunboats could glide over the iron rods with several feet between, he forgot that the powder would gather moisture and the locks become rusty.

It was discovered, after a while, that the torpedoes leaked, that the powder became damp, and changed to an inky mass, and that the hundreds of thousands of dollars which Mr. Maury had spent was all wasted. Then they who had supposed him to be a scientific man said he was a humbug.

The taking of Fort Donelson compelled the Rebels to evacuate Columbus,—the Gibraltar of the Mississippi, as they called it,—and all the work which had been done was of no benefit. Nashville was evacuated on the 27th of February. On the 4th of March Commodore Foote, having seen signs that the Rebels were leaving Columbus, went down the river, with six gunboats, accompanied by several transports, with troops, under General Sherman, to see about it. The *Cincinnati*, having been repaired, was the flag-ship. Commodore Foote requested me to accompany him, if I desired to.

"Perhaps we shall have hot work," he said, as I stepped on board in the evening of the 3rd.

"We shall move at four o'clock," said Captain Stemble, commanding the ship, "and shall be at Columbus at daybreak."

It was a new and strange experience, that first night on a gunboat, with some probability that at daybreak I might be under a hot fire from a hundred Rebel guns. By the dim light of the lamp I could see the great gun within six feet of me, and shining cutlasses and gleaming muskets. Looking out of the ward-room, I could see the men in their hammocks asleep, like orioles in their hanging nests. The sentinels paced the deck above, and all was silent but the sound of the great wheel of the steamer turning lazily in the stream, and the gurgling of the water around the bow.

"We are approaching Columbus," said an officer. It was still some time to sunrise, but the men were all astir. Their hammocks were packed away. They were clearing the decks for action, running out the guns, bringing up shot and shell, tugging and pulling at the ropes. Going on deck, I could see in the dim light the outline of the bluff at Columbus. Far up stream were dark clouds of smoke from the other steamers.

Commodore Foote was on the upper deck, walking with crutches, still lame from the wound received at Donelson.

"I always feel an exhilaration of spirits before going into a fight. I don't like to see men killed; but when I have a duty to perform for my country, like this, all of my energies are engaged," said the Commodore.

Right opposite, on the Missouri shore, was the Belmont battle-ground, where General Grant fought his first battle, and where the gunboats saved the army.

There was a house riddled with cannon-shot; there was a hole in the roof as big as a bushel-basket, where the shell went in, and in the gable an opening large enough for the passage of a cart and oxen, where it came out. It exploded, and tore the end of the building to pieces.

One by one the boats came down. The morning brightened. We could see men on the bluff, and a flag flying. Were the Rebels there? We could not make out the flag. We dropped a little nearer. More men came in sight.

"Four companies of cavalry were sent out from Paducah on a reconnaissance day before yesterday. Perhaps the Rebels have all gone, and they are in possession of the place," said General Sherman.

"I will make a reconnaissance with a party of soldiers," he added. He jumped on board his tug, and went off to get his soldiers.

"Captain Phelps, you will please to take my tug and drop down also," said Commodore Foote. "If you are willing to run the risk, you are at liberty to accompany Captain Phelps," were his words to me. What is a thing worth that costs nothing?

We drop down the stream slowly and cautiously.

"We are in easy range. If the Rebels are there, they could trouble us," says Captain Phelps.

We drop nearer. The flag is still waving. The man holding it swings his hat.

They are not Rebels, but Union cavalry! Away we dash. The other tug, with General Sherman, is close behind.

"A little more steam! Lay her in quick!" says Captain Phelps.

He is not to be beaten. We jump ashore, scramble up the bank ahead of all the soldiers, reach the upper works, and fling out the Stars and Stripes to the bright morning sunshine on the abandoned works of the Rebel Gibraltar!

The crews of the boats crowd the upper decks, and send up their joyous shouts. The soldiers farther up stream give their wild hurrahs. Around us are smoking ruins,—burned barracks and storehouses, barrels of flour and bacon simmering in the fire. There are piles of shot and shell. The great chain has broken by its own weight. At the landing are hundreds of Mr. Maury's torpedoes,—old iron now. We wander over the town, along the fortifications, view the strong defences, and wonder that the Rebels gave it up,—defended as it was by one hundred and twenty guns,—without a struggle, but the fall of Fort Donelson compelled them to evacuate the place. They carried off about half of the guns, and tumbled many of those they left behind down the embankment into the river. The force which had fled numbered about sixteen thousand. Five thousand went down the river on steamboats, and the others were sent to Corinth on the cars.

This abandonment of Columbus freed Kentucky of Rebel troops. It had been invaded about six months, and Jeff Davis hoped to secure it as one of the Confederate States, but he was disappointed in his expectations. The majority of the people in that noble State could not be induced to go out of the Union.

CHAPTER 10

# Operations at New Madrid

There are many islands in the Mississippi, so many that the river pilots have numbered them from Cairo to New Orleans. The first is just below Cairo. No. 10 is about sixty miles below, where the river makes a sharp curve, sweeping round a tongue of land towards the west and northwest, then turning again at New Madrid, making a great bend towards the southeast, as you will see by the map. The island is less than a mile long, and not more than a fourth of a mile wide. It is ten or fifteen feet above high-water mark. The line between Kentucky and Tennessee strikes the river here. The current runs swiftly past the island, and steamboats descending the stream are carried within a stone's throw of the Tennessee shore. The bank on that side of the stream is also about fifteen or twenty feet above high water.

The Rebels, before commencing their works at Columbus, saw that Island No. 10 was a very strong position, and commenced fortifications there. When they evacuated Columbus, they retired to that place, and remounted the guns which they had brought away on the island and on the Tennessee shore. They thought it was a place which could not be taken. They held New Madrid, eight miles below, on the Missouri side, which was defended by two forts. They held the island and the Tennessee shore. East of their position, on the Tennessee shore, was Reelfoot Lake, a large body of water surrounded by hundreds of acres of impassable swamp, which extended across to the lower bend, preventing an approach by the Union troops from the interior of the State upon their flank. The garrison at the island, and in the batteries along the shore, had to depend upon steamboats for their supplies.

The distance across the lower promontory from the island to Tiptonville, along the border of Reelfoot Lake, is about five miles, but the distance from the island by the river to Tiptonville is over twenty miles.

On the 22d of February, General Pope, with several thousand men, left the little town of Commerce, which is above Cairo, on the Mississippi, for New Madrid, which is forty miles distant. It was a slow, toilsome march. The mud was very deep, and he could move scarcely five miles a day, but he reached New Madrid on the 3d of March, the day on which we raised the flag on the heights at Columbus.

The Rebels had completed their forts. The one above the town mounted fourteen heavy guns, and the one below it seven. Both were strong works, with bastions and angles, and ditches that could be swept by an enfilading fire. There was a line of entrenchments between the two forts, enclosing the town.

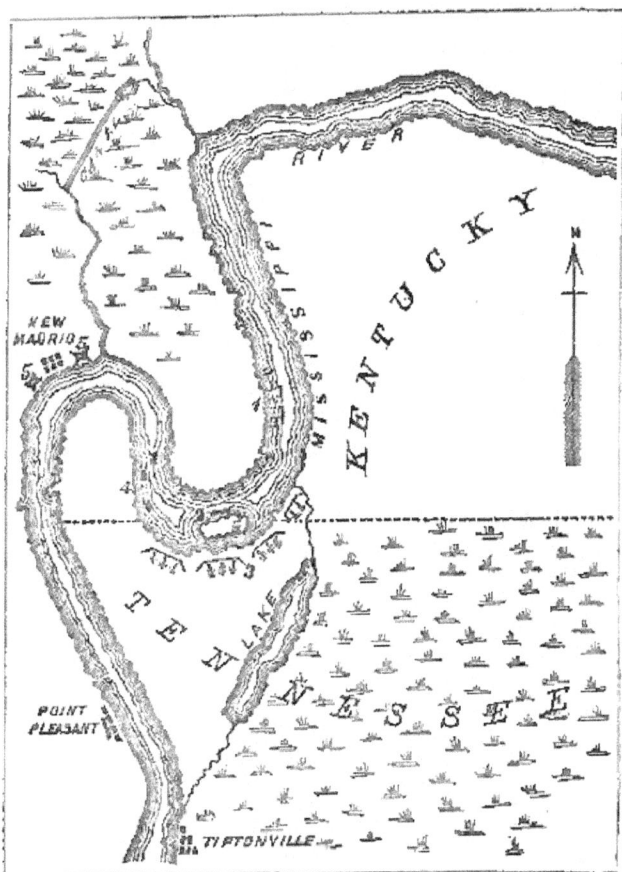

ISLAND No. 10.

1 Commodore Foote's fleet.          4 Rebel boats.
2 Island No. 10 and Rebel floating-battery.   5 5 Forts at New Madrid.
3 Shore batteries.

There were five regiments of infantry and several batteries of artillery, commanded by General McCown, at New Madrid. General Mackall was sent up by Beauregard to direct the defence there and at Island No. 10. When he arrived, he issued an address to the soldiers. He said:

> Soldiers: We are strangers, commander and commanded, each to the other. Let me tell you who I am. I am a General made by Beauregard,—a General selected by Beauregard and Bragg for this command, when they knew it was in peril.
>
> They have known me for twenty years; together we stood on the fields of Mexico. Give them your confidence now; give it to me when I have earned it.
>
> Soldiers: The Mississippi Valley is entrusted to your courage, to your discipline, to your patience; exhibit the coolness and vigilance you have heretofore, and hold it.[23]

They thought they could hold the place. A Rebel officer wrote, on the 11th of March, to his friends thus:

> General Mackall has put the rear in effective defence. The forts are impregnable. All are hopeful and ready. We will make this an American Thermopylae, if necessary.[24]

By this he intended to say that they would all die before they would surrender the place, and would make New Madrid as famous in history as that narrow mountain-pass in Greece, where the immortal three hundred under Leonidas fought the Persian host.

The Rebels had several gunboats on the river, each carrying three or four guns. The river was very high, and its banks overflowed. The country is level for miles around, and it was an easy matter for the gunboats to throw shells over the town into the woods upon General Pope's army. The Rebels had over sixty pieces of heavy artillery, while General Pope had only his light field artillery; but he sent to Cairo for siege-guns, meanwhile driving in the enemy's pickets and investing the place.

He detached Colonel Plummer, of the Eleventh Missouri, with three regiments and a battery of rifled Parrott guns, to take possession of Point Pleasant, ten miles farther down. The order was admirably executed. Colonel Plummer planted his guns, threw up entrenchments, and astonished the Rebels by sending his shells into a steamboat which was passing up with supplies.

---

23: *Rebellion Record.*
24: *Memphis Appeal.*

Commodore Hollins, commanding the Rebel gunboats, made all haste down to find out what was going on. He rained shot and shell all day long upon Colonel Plummer's batteries, but could not drive him from the position he had selected. He had made holes in the ground for his artillery, and the Rebel shot did him no injury. Hollins began at long range, then steamed up nearer to the batteries, but Plummer's artillerymen, by their excellent aim, compelled him to withdraw. The next day Hollins tried it again, but with no better success. The river was effectually blockaded. No Rebel transport could get up, and those which were at Island No. 10 and New Madrid could not get down, without being subjected to a heavy fire.

General Mackall determined to hold New Madrid, and reinforced the place from Island No. 10, till he had about nine thousand troops. On the 11th of March four siege-guns were sent to General Pope. He received them at sunset. Colonel Morgan's brigade was furnished with spades and entrenching tools. General Stanley's division was ordered under arms, to support Morgan. The force advanced towards the town at dark, drove in the Rebel pickets, secured a favourable position within eight hundred yards of the fort. The men worked all night, and in the morning had two breastworks thrown up, each eighteen feet thick, and five feet high, with a smaller breastwork, called a curtain, connecting the two. This curtain was nine hundred feet long, nine feet thick, and three feet high. On each side of the breastworks, thrown out like wings was a line of rifle-pits. Wooden platforms were placed behind the breastworks, and the guns all mounted by daylight. Colonel Bissell, of the engineers, managed it all. In thirty-four hours from the time he received the guns at Cairo, he had shipped them across the Mississippi River, loaded them on railroad cars, taken them to Sykestown, twenty miles, mounted them on carriages, then dragged them twenty miles farther, through almost impassable mud, and had them in position within eight hundred yards of the river! The work was done so quietly that the Rebel pickets did not mistrust what was going on. At daybreak they opened fire upon what they supposed was a Union rifle-pit, and were answered by a shell from a rifled thirty-two pounder.

It was a foggy morning. The air was still, and the deep thunder rolled far away along the wooded stream. It woke up the slumbering garrison. Commodore Hollins heard it, and immediately there was commotion among the Rebel gunboats. They came to New Madrid. Hollins placed them in position above the town to open fire. The fog lifted, and all the guns of the fleet and the forts began to play upon the breastworks. General Pope brought up his heavy field guns, and replied. He paid but little attention to the fort, but sent his shot and shell at the gunboats. Captain Mower, of the First United States artillery, commanded the batteries, and his fire was so accurate that the gunboats were obliged to take new positions. Shortly after the cannonade began, a shot from the fort struck one of Captain Mower's thirty-two pounders in the muzzle and disabled it; but he kept up his fire through the day, dismounting three guns in the lower fort and disabling two of the gunboats. Nearly all of the shells from the Rebel batteries fell harmlessly into the soft earth. There were very few of General Pope's men injured. They soon became accustomed to the business, and paid but little attention to the screaming of the shot and the explosions of the shells. They had many hearty laughs, as the shells which burst in the ground frequently spattered them with mud.

There was one soldier in one of the Ohio regiments who was usually profane and wicked; but he was deeply impressed with the fact that so few were injured by such a terrific fire, and at night said to his comrades, seriously: "Boys, there is no use denying it; God has watched over us to-day."

His comrades also noticed that he did not swear that night.

Just at night, General Paine's division made a demonstration towards the lower fort, driving in the enemy's pickets. General Paine advanced almost to the ditch in front of the fort. Preparations were made to hold the ground, but during the night there came up a terrific thunder-storm and hurricane, which stopped all operations.

The Twenty-seventh and Thirty-ninth Ohio, and the Tenth and Sixteenth Illinois, were the grand guard for the night. They had been under fire all day. They had endured the strain upon their nerves, but through the long night-hours they stood in the drenching rain, beneath the sheets of lurid flame, looking with sleepless eyes towards the front, prepared to repel a sortie or challenge spies.

At daybreak there was no enemy in sight. The fort was deserted. A citizen of the town came out with a flag of truce. The General who had called upon his men in high-sounding words, the officer who was going to make New Madrid a Thermopylae, and himself a Leonidas in history,—the nine thousand infantry had gone! Two or three soldiers were found asleep. They rubbed their eyes and stared wildly when they were told that they were prisoners, that their comrades and commander had fled.

During the thunder-storm, the Rebel gunboats and steamers had taken the troops on board, and ferried them to the Tennessee shore near Island No. 10. They spiked their heavy guns, but Colonel Bissell's engineers were quickly at work, and in a few hours had the guns ready for use again.

The Rebels left an immense amount of corn, in bags, and a great quantity of ammunition. They tumbled their wagons into the river.

General Pope set his men to work, and before night the guns which had been pointed inland were wheeled the other way. He sent a messenger to Commodore Foote, with this despatch:

All right! River closed! No escape for the enemy by water.

All this was accomplished with the loss of seven killed and forty-three wounded. By these operations against New Madrid, and by the battle at Pea Ridge, in the south-western part of the State, which was fought about the same time, the Rebels were driven from Missouri!

CHAPTER 11

# Operations at Island Number Ten

Commodore Foote, having repaired the gunboats disabled at Fort Donelson, sailed from Cairo the day that New Madrid fell into the hands of General Pope. He had seven gunboats and ten mortars, besides several tugs and transports. Colonel Buford, with fifteen hundred troops, accompanied the expedition.

The mortars were untried. They were the largest ever brought into use at that time, weighing nineteen thousand pounds, and throwing a shell thirteen inches in diameter. The accompanying diagram will perhaps give you an idea of their appearance. You see the mortar mounted on its carriage, or bed as it is called. The figures 1, 1 represent one cheek of the bed, a thick wrought-iron plate. The figures 2, 2 represent the heads of the bolts which connect the cheek in view to the one on the other side. The bed stands on thick timbers, represented by 3, and the timbers rest on heavy sleepers, 4. Figure 5 represents a thick strap of iron which clasps the trunion or axis of the mortar, and holds it in its place. This strap is held by two other straps, 6, 6, all iron, and very strong. The figure 7 represents what is called a bolster. You see it is in the shape of a wedge. It is used to raise or depress the muzzle of the mortar. The figure 8 represents what is called a quoin, and keeps the bolster in its place. The figure 9 represents one of the many bolts by which the whole is kept in place on the boat.

The boat is built like a raft, of thick timbers, laid crosswise and bolted firmly together. It is about thirty feet long and twelve wide, and has iron plates around its sides to screen the men from Rebel sharpshooters. The mortar is more than four feet in diameter. It is thicker than it is long. To fire a mortar accurately requires a good knowledge of mathematics, of the relations of curves to straight lines, for the shell is fired into the air at an angle of thirty or forty degrees. The gunner

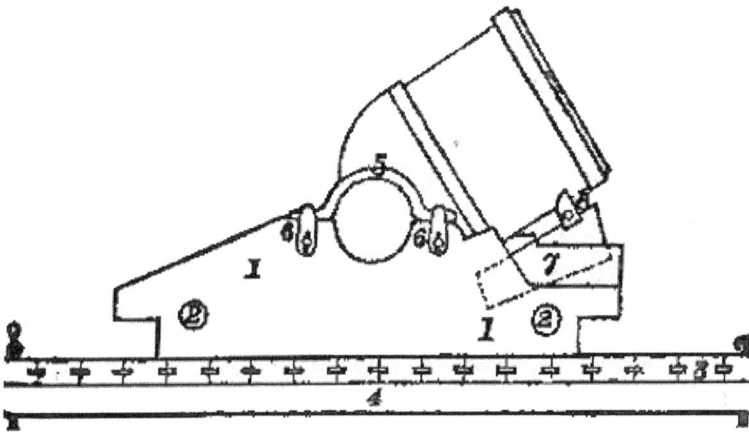

A MORTAR.

must calculate the distance from the mortar to the enemy in a straight line, and then elevate or lower the muzzle to drop his shell not too near, neither too far away. He must calculate the time it will take for the shell to describe the curve through the air. Then he must make his fuses of the right length to have the shell explode at the proper time, either high in the air, that its fragments may rain down on the encampment of the enemy, or close down to the ground among the men working the guns. It requires skill and a great deal of practice to do all this.

The mortar flotilla was commanded by Captain Henry E. Maynadier, assisted by Captain E. B. Pike of the engineers. There were four Masters of Ordnance, who commanded each four mortars. Each mortar-boat had a crew of fifteen men; three of them were Mississippi flatboatmen, who understood all about the river, the currents and the sand-bars.

Commodore Foote's flotilla consisted of the *Benton*, 16 guns, which was his flag-ship, covered all over with iron plates, and commanded by Captain Phelps; the *Mound City*, 13 guns, commanded by Captain Kelty; the *Carondelet*, 13 guns, Lieutenant Walke; the *Cincinnati*, 13 guns, Captain Stemble; the *St. Louis*, 13 guns, Captain Dove; the *Louisville*, 13 guns, Lieutenant Paulding; the *Pittsburg*, 13 guns, Lieutenant Thompson; the *Conestoga*, 9 guns, Lieutenant Blodgett; in all, 103 guns and 10 mortars. The *Conestoga* was used to guard the ammunition-boats, and took no part in the active operations. Commodore Foote had several small steam-tugs, which were used as tenders, to carry orders from boat to boat.

The Southern people thought that Island No. 10 could not be taken. On the 6th of March a newspaper at Memphis said:

> For the enemy to get possession of Memphis and the Mississippi Valley would require an army of greater strength than Secretary Stanton can concentrate upon the banks of the Mississippi River. The gunboats in which they have so much confidence have proved their weakness. They cannot stand our guns of heavy calibre. The approach of the enemy by land to New Madrid induces us to believe that the flotilla is one grand humbug, and that it is not ready, and does not intend to descend the river. Foote, the commander of the Federal fleet, served his time under Commodore Hollins, and should he attempt to descend the river, Hollins will teach him that some things can be done as well as others.[25]

On Saturday, the 15th of March, the fleet approached the island. The clouds were thick and lowering. The rain pattered on the decks of the gunboats, the fog settled upon the river. As the boats swept round a point of land, the old river pilot, who was on the watch, who knew every crook, turn, sand-bar, and all the objects along the bank, sung out, "Boat ahead!"

The sailors scrambled to the portholes; Captain Phelps sprang from the cabin to the deck.

There she was, a steamer, just visible through the fog a mile ahead. It was the Grampus, owned by Captain Chester of the steamer Alps, who had two of the mortar-boats in tow. He belonged to Pittsburg, and used to carry coal to Memphis. When the war broke out the Rebels seized his steamboats and his coal-barges, and refused to pay him for the coal they had already purchased. The act roused all his ire. He was a tall, athletic man, and had followed the river thirty years. Although surrounded by enemies, he gave them plain words.

"You are a set of thieves and rascals! You are cowards, every one of you!" he shouted.

He took off his coat, rolled up his shirt-sleeves, bared his great brawny arms, dashed his hat upon the ground.

"Now come on! I'll fight every one of you, you infernal rascals! I'll whip you all! I challenge you to fight me! You call yourselves chivalrous people. You say you believe in fair play. If I whip, you shall give up my boats, but if I am beaten, you are welcome to them."

---

25: *Memphis Argus.*

They laughed in his face, and said: "Blow away, old fellow. We have got your boats. Help yourself if you can."

A hot-headed secessionist cried out, "Hang the Yankee!"

The crowd hustled him about, but he had a few old friends, who took his part, and he succeeded in making his escape.

Captain Phelps looked a moment at the *Grampus*. He saw her wheels move. She was starting off.

"Out with the starboard gun! Give her a shot!"

Lieutenant Bishop runs his eye along the sights of the great eleven-inch gun, which has been loaded and run out of the porthole in a twinkling.

There is a flash. A great cloud puffs out into the fog, and the shot screams through the air and is lost to sight. We cannot see where it fell. Another—another. Boom!—boom!—boom!—from the *Cincinnati* and *Carondelet*. But the *Grampus* is light-heeled. The distance widens. You can hardly see her, and at last she vanishes like a ghost from sight.

We were not more than four or five miles from the head of the island. One by one the boats rounded to along the Kentucky shore. The sailors sprang upon the land, carrying out the strong warps, and fastening us to the trunks of the buttonwood-trees.

There was a clearing and a miserable log-hut near by. The family had fled, frightened by the cannonade. We found them cowering in the woods,—a man, his wife and daughter. The land all around them was exceedingly rich, but they were very poor. All they had to eat was hog and hominy. They had been told that the Union troops would rob them of all they had, which was not likely, because they had nothing worth stealing! They were trembling with fear, but when they found the soldiers and sailors well-behaved and peaceable, they forgot their terror.

The fog lifts at last, and we can see the white tents of the Rebels on the Tennessee shore. There are the batteries, with the cannon grim and black pointing up stream. Round the point of land is the island. A half-dozen steamboats lie in the stream below it. At times they steam up to the bend and then go back again,—wandering back and forth like rats in a cage. They cannot get past General Pope's guns at New Madrid. On the north side of the island is a great floating-battery of eight guns, which has been towed up from New Orleans. General Mackall has sunk a steamboat in a narrow part of the channel on the north side of the island, so that if Commodore Foote attempts to run the blockade he will be compelled to pass along the south channel, exposed to the fire of all the guns in the four batteries upon the Tennessee shore, as well as those upon the island.

Two of the mortar-boats were brought into position two miles from the Rebel batteries. We waited in a fever of expectation while Captain Maynadier was making ready, for thirteen-inch mortars had never been used in war. The largest used by the French and English in the bombardment of Sebastopol were much smaller.

There came a roar like thunder. It was not a sharp, piercing report, but a deep, heavy boom, which rolled along the mighty river, echoing and re-echoing from shore to shore,—a prolonged reverberation, heard fifty miles away. A keg of powder was burned in the single explosion. The shell rose in a beautiful curve, exploded five hundred feet high, and fell in fragments around the distant encampment.

There was a flash beneath the dark forest-trees near the encampment, a puff of white smoke, an answering roar, and a shot fell into the water a half-mile down stream from the mortars. The Rebels had accepted the challenge.

Sunday came. The boats having the mortars in tow dropped them along the Missouri shore. The gunboats swung into the stream. The *Benton* fired her rifled guns over the point of land at the Rebel steamboats below the island. There was a sudden commotion. They quickly disappeared down the river towards New Madrid, out of range. During the morning there was a deep booming from the direction of Point Pleasant. The Rebel gunboats were trying to drive Colonel Plummer from his position.

Ten o'clock came, the hour for divine service. The church flag was flung out on the flagstaff of the *Benton*, and all the commanders called their crews together for worship. I was on board the *Pittsburg* with Captain Thompson. The crew assembled on the upper deck. There were men from Maine, New Hampshire, Massachusetts, and Rhode Island, from the Eastern as well as the Western States. Some of them were scholars and teachers in Sabbath-schools at home. They were dressed in dark-blue, and each sailor appeared in his Sunday suit. A small table was brought up from the cabin, and the flag of our country spread upon it. A Bible was brought. We stood around the captain with uncovered heads, while he read the twenty-seventh Psalm. Beautiful and appropriate was that service:

*The Lord is my light and my salvation; whom shall I fear?*
*The Lord is the strength of my life; of whom shall I be afraid?*
After the Psalm, the prayer, *"Our Father which art in heaven."*

How impressive! The uncovered group standing around the open Bible, and the low voices of a hundred men in prayer. On our right hand, looking down the mighty river, were the mortars, in play, jarring the earth with their heavy thunders. The shells were sweeping in graceful curves through the air. Upon our left hand, the *Benton* and *Carondelet* were covering themselves with white clouds, which slowly floated away over the woodlands, fragrant with the early buds and blossoms of spring. The Rebel batteries below us were flaming and smoking. Solid shot screamed past us, shells exploded above us. Away beyond the island, beyond the dark-green of the forest, rose the cloud of another bombardment, where Commodore Hollins was vainly endeavouring to drive Colonel Plummer from his position. So the prayer was mingled with the deep, wild thunders of the cannonade.

A light fog, like a thin veil, lay along the river. After service, we saw that strange and peculiar optical illusion called *mirage*, so often seen in deserts, where the thirsty traveller beholds lakes, and shady places, cities, towns, and ships. I was looking up stream, and saw, sweeping round the wooded point of land, something afloat. A boat or floating battery it seemed to be. There were chimneys, a flagstaff, a porthole. It was seemingly two hundred feet long, coming broadside towards us.

"Captain Thompson, see there!"

He looked at it, and jumped upon the pilot-house, scanned it over and over. The other officers raised their glasses.

"It looks like a floating battery!" said one.

"There is a porthole, certainly!" said another.

It came nearer. Its proportions increased.

"Pilot, put on steam! Head her up stream!" said Captain Thompson.

"Lieutenant, beat to quarters! Light up the magazine! We will see what she is made of."

There was activity on deck. The guns were run out, shot and shell were brought up. The boat moved up stream. Broadside upon us came the unknown craft.

Suddenly the illusion vanished. The monster three hundred feet long, changed to an old coal-barge. The chimneys became two timbers, the flagstaff a small stick of firewood. The fog, the currents of air, had produced the transformation. We had a hearty laugh over our preparations for an encounter with the enemy in our rear. It was an enemy more quickly disposed of than the one in front.

The Rebels in the upper battery waved a white flag. The firing ceased.

Commodore Foote sent Lieutenant Bishop down with a tug and a white flag flying, to see what it meant. He approached the battery.

"Are we to understand that you wish to communicate with us?" he asked.

"No, sir," said an officer wearing a gold-laced coat.

"Then why do you display a white flag?"

"It is a mistake, sir. It is a signal-flag. I regret that it has deceived you."

"Good morning, sir."

"Good morning, sir."

The tug steams back to the *Benton*, the white flag is taken down, and the uproar begins again. Lieutenant Bishop made good use of his eyes. There were seven thirty-two-pounders and one heavy rifled gun in the upper battery.

Commodore Foote was not ready to begin the bombardment in earnest till Monday noon, March 17th.

The *Benton, Cincinnati*, and *St. Louis* dropped down stream, side by side, and came into position about a mile from the upper batteries. Anchors were dropped from the stern of each gunboat, that they might fight head on, using their heavy rifled guns. Their position was on the east side of the river. The *Mound City* and *Carondelet* took position near the west bank, just below the mortars. The boats were thus placed to bring a cross fire upon the upper Rebel battery.

"Pay no attention to the island, but direct your fire into the upper battery!" is the order.

A signal is raised upon the flag-ship. We do not understand the signification of the flag, but while we look at it the ten mortars open fire, one after another, in rapid succession. The gunboats follow. There are ten shells, thirteen inches in diameter, rising high in air. There are handfuls of smoke flecking the sky, and a prolonged, indescribable crashing, rolling, and rumbling. You have seen battle-pieces by the great painters; but the highest artistic skill cannot portray the scene. It is a vernal day, as beautiful as ever dawned. The gunboats are enveloped in flame and smoke. The unfolding clouds are slowly wafted away by the gentle breeze. Huge columns rise majestically from the mortars. A line of white—a thread-like tissue—spans the sky. It is the momentary and vanishing mark of the shell in the invisible air. There are little splashes in the stream, where the fragments of iron fall. There are pillars of water tossed upward in front of the earthwork, which break into spray, painted with rainbow hues by the bright sunshine. A round shot skips along the surface and pierces the embankment. Another just clears the parapet, and cuts down a tree beyond. The air is filled with sticks, timbers, branches of trees, and earth, as if a dozen thunderbolts had fallen upon the spot from a cloudless sky. There are explosions deep under ground, where the great shells have buried themselves in their downward flight. There are volumes of smoke which rise like the mists of a summer morning.

There are some brave fellows behind that breastwork. Amid this storm they come out from their shelter and load a gun. There it comes! A flash, a cloud, a hissing, a crash! The shot strikes the upper deck of the *Benton*, tears up the iron plates, breaks the thick timbers into kindlings, falls upon the lower deck, bounds up again to the beams above, and drops into Commodore Foote's writing-desk!

All around, from the gunboats, the mortars, from all the batteries, are flashes, clouds of smoke, and thunderings, which bring to mind the gorgeous imagery of the Book of Revelation in the New Testament, descriptive of the scenes of the Last Judgment.

The firing ceased at sunset. The *Benton* was struck four times, and the *Cincinnati* once. No one was injured by these shots, but one of the guns of the *St. Louis* burst, killing two men instantly, and wounding thirteen.

When the bombardment was at its height, Commodore Foote received a letter from Cairo, containing the sad information that a beloved son had died suddenly. It was a sore bereavement, but it was no time for him to give way to grief, no time to think of his great affliction.

After the firing had ceased, I sat with him in the cabin of the *Benton*. There were tears upon his cheeks. He was thinking of his loss.

Were he living now, I should have no right to give the conversation I had with him, but he has gone to his reward, leaving us his bright example. These were his words, as I remember:—

"It is a terrible blow, but the Lord gave, and the Lord hath taken away; blessed be His name. It is hard for me to bear, but no harder than it will be for the fathers of the noble men who were killed on the *St. Louis*. Poor fellows! I feel bad for the wounded."

He called the orderly who stood outside the cabin.

"Orderly, tell the surgeon that I want to see him."

The surgeon came in.

"Surgeon, I wish you to do everything you can for those poor fellows on the *St. Louis*. Don't omit anything that will contribute to their comfort."

"It shall be done, sir," said the surgeon, as he left the cabin.

"Poor fellows! I must see them myself. It is a great deal worse to have a gun explode than to have the men wounded by the enemy's shot, for they lose confidence. I have protested again and again to the Department against using these old thirty-two-pounders, which have been weakened by being rifled; but I had to take them or none. I had to pick them up wherever I could find them. I have tried my best to get the fleet in good trim, and it is too bad to have the men slaughtered in this way. I shall try to do my duty. The country needs the services of every man. We shall have a long war. I would like to rest, and have a little breathing spell, but I shall not ask for it. I shall try to do my duty to my country and to God. He is leading this nation in a way we know not of. My faith is unshaken in Him. He will bring us out of all trouble at last."

Thus, in the hour of battle, while attending to his duties, while bearing up under the intelligence that a beloved son had died, he talked calmly, cheerfully, and hopefully of the future, and manifested the care and tenderness of a father for the wounded.

Although the gunboats ceased firing at sunset, the mortars were in play all night. It was beautiful to see the great flash, illuminating all the landscape, the white cloud rolling upward and outward, unfolding, expanding, spreading over the wide river, and the bright spark rising high in the air, turning with the revolving shell, reaching its altitude and sailing straight along the arch of the parabola, then descending with increasing rapidity, ending in a bright flash, and an explosion which echoes and re-echoes far away. The next day I went with Captain Maynadier across the point to reconnoitre the batteries on the island and watch the explosions of the shells. We passed a deserted farm-house, and saw a squad of Colonel Buford's soldiers running down pigs and chickens. Crossing a creek upon a corduroy bridge, we came to a second squad. One was playing a violin, and several were dancing; they were as happy as larks. We stood upon the bank of the river opposite the island. Before us was the floating battery, which was formerly the New Orleans dry-dock. It mounted eight guns. There were four batteries on the Tennessee shore and several on the island. We could see the artillerists at their guns. They saw us, and sent a shell whizzing over our heads, which struck in a cornfield, and ploughed a deep furrow for the farmer owning it. We went where they could not see us, and mounted a fence to watch the effect of the mortar-firing. It was interesting to sit there and hear the great shells sail through the air five hundred feet above us. It was like the sound of far-off, invisible machinery, turning with a constant motion, not the sharp, shrill whistle of a rifled-bolt, but a whirr and roll, like that which you may sometimes hear above the clouds in a thunder-storm. One shell fell like a millstone into the river. The water did not extinguish the fuse, and a great column was thrown up fifty feet high. Another buried itself deep in the ground before it burst, and excavated a great hole. I learned, after the place surrendered, that one fell through a tent where several officers were sitting, playing cards, and that the next moment the tent, furniture, officers, and fifty cartloads of earth were sailing through the air! None of them were wounded, but they were bruised, wrenched, and their nice clothes covered with dirt.

At night there was a storm, with vivid lightning and heavy thunder. The mortars kept up their fire. It was a sublime spectacle,—earth against heaven, but the artillery of the skies was the best.

You would have given a great deal, I dare say, to have seen all this; but there is another side to the story. Can you eat dirt? Can you eat grease in all its forms,—baked, boiled, fried, simmered? Can you bear variegated butter, variable in taste and smell? Can you get along with ham, hash, and beans for breakfast, beans, hash, and ham for dinner, and hash, ham, and beans for supper, week after week, with fat in all its forms, with cakes solid enough for grape-shot to fire at the Rebels, with blackest coffee and the nearest available cow fifty miles off?—with sour molasses, greasy griddle-cakes, with Mississippi water thick with the filth of the great valley of the West, with slime from the Cincinnati slaughter-houses, sweepings from the streets, slops from the steamboats, with all the miasma and mould of the forests? The fairest countenance soon changes to a milk and molasses colour, and energy lags, and strength becomes weakness under such living.

In boyhood, at the sound of a bugle, a drum, or the roar of a cannon, how leaped the blood through my veins! But it becomes an old story. I was quartered within a stone's-throw of the mortars, which fired all night long, and was not disturbed by the explosions. One becomes indifferent to everything. You get tired of watching the cannonade, and become so accustomed to the fire of the enemy, that after a while you do not heed a shot that ploughs up the dirt or strikes the water near at hand.

General Pope sent word, that, if he had transports and a gunboat, he could cross to the Tennessee shore and take the batteries in the rear. The river was very high and the country overflowed. Near New

Madrid there is a bayou, which is the outlet of a small lake. It was determined to cut a canal through the forest to the lake. Colonel Bissell with his regiment of engineers went to work. Four steamboats were fitted up, two barges, with cannon on board, were taken in tow, and the expedition started. They sailed over a cornfield, where the tall stalks were waving and swinging in the water, steamed over fences, and came to the woods. There were great trees, which must be cut away. The engineers rigged their saws for work under water. The path was fifty feet wide and the trees were cut off four feet below the surface. In eight days they cut their way to New Madrid, a distance of twelve miles. In one place they cut off seventy-five trees, all of which were more than two feet in diameter.

While this was doing, Commodore Foote kept the Rebels awake by a regular and continuous bombardment, mainly upon the upper battery. He determined to capture it.

On the night of the 1st of April, an armed expedition is fitted out from the squadron and the land forces. There are five boats, manned by picked crews from the gunboats, carrying forty men of the Forty-second Illinois, under command of Colonel Roberts. The party numbers one hundred. It is a wild night. The wind blows a gale from the south, swaying the great trees of the forest and tossing up waves upon the swift-running river, which boils, bubbles, dashes, and foams in the storm. There are vivid lightning flashes, growls and rolls of deep, heavy thunder. The boats cast off from the fleet. The oars have been muffled. No words are spoken. The soldiers sit, each with his gun half raised to his shoulder and his hand upon the lock. The spray dashes over them, sheets of flame flash in their faces. All the landscape for a moment is as light as day, and then all is pitch darkness.

Onward faster and faster they sweep, driven by the strong arms of the rowers and the current. It is a stealthy, noiseless, rapid, tempestuous, dangerous, daring enterprise. They are tossed by the waves, but they glide with the rapidity of a race-horse. Two sentinels stand upon the parapet. A few rods in rear is a regiment of Rebels. A broad lightning-flash reveals the descending boats. The sentinels fire their guns, but they are mimic flashes.

"Lay in quick!" shouts Colonel Roberts.

The oars bend in the row-locks. A stroke, and they are beside the parapet, climbing up the slippery bank. The sentinels run. There is a rattling fire from pistols and muskets; but the shots fall harmlessly in the forest. A moment,—and all the guns are spiked. There is a commotion in the woods. The sleeping Rebels are astir. They do not rally to drive back the invaders, but are fleeing in the darkness.

Colonel Roberts walks from gun to gun, to see if the work has been effectually accomplished.

"All right! All aboard! Push off!" He is the last to leave. The boats head up-stream. The rowers bend to their oars. In a minute they are beyond musket range. Their work is accomplished, and there will be no more firing from that six-gun battery. Now the gunboats can move nearer and begin their work upon the remaining batteries.

In the morning General Mackall was much chagrined when he found out what had been done by the Yankees. It is said he used some hard words. He flew into a rage, and grew red in the face, which did not help the matter in the least.

At midnight, on the night of the 3d of April, the *Carondelet*, commanded by Captain Walke, ran past the batteries and the island. It was a dark, stormy night. But the sentinels saw her coming down in the darkness, and every cannon was brought to bear upon the vessel. Shells burst around her; solid shot, grape, and canister swept over her; but she was not struck, although exposed to the terrific fire over thirty minutes. We who remained with the fleet waited in breathless suspense to hear her three signal-guns, which were to be fired if she passed safely. They came,—boom! boom! boom! She was safe. We cheered, hurrahed, and lay down to sleep, to dream it all over again.

The *Carondelet* reached New Madrid. The soldiers of General Pope's army rushed to the bank, and gave way to the wildest enthusiasm.

"Three cheers for the *Carondelet!*" shouted one. Their caps went into the air, they swung their arms, and danced in ecstasy.

"Three more for Commodore Foote!"

"Now three more for Captain Walke!"

"Three more for the Navy!"

"Three more for the Cabin-Boy!"

So they went on cheering and shouting for everything till they were hoarse.

The next day the *Carondelet* went down the river as far as Point Pleasant, had an engagement with several batteries on the Tennessee shore, silenced them, landed and spiked the guns. The next night the *Pittsburg*, Captain Thompson ran the blockade safely. The four steamboats which had worked their way through the canal were all ready. The Tenth, Sixteenth, Twenty-first, and Fifty-first Illinois regiments were taken on board. The Rebels had a heavy battery on the other side of the river, at a place called Watson's Landing. The *Carondelet* and *Pittsburg* went ahead, opened fire, and silenced it. The steamers advanced. The Rebels saw the preparations and fled towards Tiptonville. By midnight General Pope had all his troops on the Tennessee shore. General Paine, commanding those in advance, pushed on towards Tiptonville and took possession of all the deserted camps. The Rebels had fled in confusion, casting away their guns, knapsacks, clothing, everything, to escape. When the troops in the batteries heard what was going on in their rear, they also fled towards Tiptonville. General Pope came up with them the next morning and captured all who had not escaped. General Mackall and two other generals, nearly seven thousand prisoners, one hundred and twenty-three pieces of artillery, seven thousand small arms, and an immense amount of ammunition and supplies fell into the hands of General Pope. The troops on the island, finding that they were deserted, surrendered to Commodore Foote. It was almost a bloodless victory, but one of great importance, opening the Mississippi River down to Fort Pillow, forty miles above Memphis.

When the State of Tennessee was carried out of the Union by the treachery of Governor Harris, and other men in high official position, there were some men in the western part of the State, as well as the eastern, who remained loyal. Those who were suspected of loving the Union suffered terrible persecutions. Among them was a citizen of Purdy. His name was Hurst. He told me the story of his wrongs.

Soon after the State seceded, he was visited by a number of men who called themselves a vigilance committee. They were fierce-looking fellows, armed with pistols and knives.

"We want you to come with us," said the leader of the gang.

"What do you want of me?"

"We will let you know when you get there."

Mr. Hurst knew that they wanted to take him before their own self-elected court, and went without hesitation.

He was questioned, but would not commit himself by any positive answer, and, as they could not prove he was in favour of the Union, they allowed him to go home.

But the ruffians were not satisfied, and in a few days had him up again. They tried hard to prove that he was opposed to the Confederacy, but he had kept about his own business, had refrained from talking, and they could not convict him. They allowed him to go for several months. One day, in September, 1861, while at work in his field, the

156

ruffians came again. Their leader had a red face, bloated with whiskey, chewed tobacco, had two pistols in his belt, and a long knife in a sheath. He wore a slouched hat, and was a villainous-looking fellow.

"Come, you scoundrel. We will fix you this time," said the captain of the band.

"What do you want of me?"

"You are an Abolitionist,—a Yankee spy. That's what you are. We'll make you stretch hemp this time," they said, seizing him and marching him into town, with their pistols cocked. Six or eight of them were ready to shoot him if he should attempt to escape. They called all who did not go for secession Abolitionists.

"I am not an Abolitionist," said Hurst.

"None of your sass. We know what you are, and if you don't hold your jaw, we will stop it for you."

They marched him through the village, and the whole population turned out to see him. He was taken to the jail, and thrust into a cage, so small that he could not lie down,—a vile, filthy place. The jailer was a brutal, hard-hearted man,—a rabid secessionist. He chuckled with delight when he turned the key on Hurst. He was kept in the cage two days, and then taken to Nashville, where he was tried before a military court.

He was charged with being opposed to the Confederacy, and in favour of the Union; also that he was a spy.

Among his accusers were some secessionists who owed him a grudge. They invented lies, swore that Hurst was in communication with the Yankees, and gave them information of all the movements of the Rebels. This was months before General Grant attacked Donelson, and Hurst was two hundred miles from the nearest post of the Union army; but such was the hatred of the secessionists, and they were so bloodthirsty, that they were ready to hang all who did not hurrah for Jeff Davis and the Confederacy. He was far from home. He was not permitted to have any witnesses, and his own word was of no value in their estimation. He was condemned to be hung as a spy.

They took him out to a tree, put the rope round his neck, when some of his old acquaintances, who were not quite so hardened as his accusers, said that the evidence was not sufficient to hang him. They took him back to the court. He came under heavy bonds to report himself often and prove his whereabouts.

He was released, and went home, but his old enemies followed him, and dogged him day and night.

He discovered that he was to be again arrested. He told his boy to harness his horse quick, and take him to a side street, near an apothecary's shop. He looked out of the window, and saw a file of soldiers approaching to arrest him. He slipped out of the back door, gained the street, and walked boldly through the town.

"There he goes!" said a fellow smoking a cigar on the steps of the hotel. A crowd rushed out of the bar-room to see him. They knew that he was to be arrested; they expected he would be hung.

As he walked into the apothecary's shop, he saw his boy coming down the alley with his horse. He did not dare to go down the alley to meet him, for the crowd would see his attempt to escape. They saw him enter the door, and rushed across the street to see the fun when the soldiers should arrive.

"Come in here," he said to the apothecary, as he stepped into a room in the rear, from which a door opened into the alley.

The apothecary followed him, wondering what he wanted.

Hurst drew a pistol from his pocket, and held it to the head of the apothecary, and said, "If you make any noise, I will blow your brains out!" He opened the door, and beckoned to his boy, who rode up. "I have four friends who are aiding me to escape," said he. "They will be the death of you if you give the alarm; but if you remain quiet, they will not harm you." He sprang upon his horse, galloped down the alley, and was gone.

The apothecary dared not give the alarm, and was very busy about his business when the soldiers came to arrest Hurst.

When they found he was gone, they started in pursuit, but were not able to overtake him. He made his way to the woods, and finally reached the Union army.

When General Lewis Wallace's division entered the town of Purdy, Hurst accompanied it. He asked General Wallace for a guard, to make an important arrest. His request was granted. He went to the jail, found the jailer, and demanded his keys. The jailer gave them up. Hurst unlocked the cage, and there he found a half-starved slave, who had been put in for no crime, but to keep him from running away to the Union army.

He released the slave and told him to go where he pleased. The coloured man could hardly stand, he was so cramped and exhausted by his long confinement and want of food.

"Step in there!" said Hurst to the jailer. The jailer shrunk back.

"Step in there, you scoundrel!" said Hurst, more determinedly.

"You don't mean to put me in there, Hurst!" said the jailer, almost whining.

"Step in, I say, or I'll let daylight through you!" He seized a gun from one of the soldiers and pricked the jailer a little with the bayonet, to let him know that he was in earnest. The other soldiers fenced him round with a glittering line of sharp steel points. They chuckled, and thought it capital fun.

The jailer stepped in, whining and begging, and saying that he never meant to harm Hurst. Having got him inside, Hurst locked the door, put the key in his pocket, dismissed the soldiers, and went away. He was gone two days, and when he returned, *had lost the key!*

The cage was built of oak logs, and bolted so firmly with iron that it took half a day, with axes, to get the jailer out. He never troubled Hurst again, who joined the Union army as a scout, and did excellent service, for he was well acquainted with the country.

While operations were going on at Island No. 10, I went up the river one day, and visited the hospitals at *Mound City* and Paducah. In one of the wards a surgeon was dressing the arm of a brave young Irishman, who was very jolly. His arm had been torn by a piece of shell, but he did not mind it much. The surgeon was performing an operation which was painful.

"Does it hurt, Patrick?" he asked.

"Ah! Doctor, ye nadent ask such a question as that; but if ye'll just give me a good drink of whiskey, ye may squeeze it all day long."

He made up such a comical face that the sick and wounded all around him laughed. It did them good, and Patrick knew it, and so, in the kindness of his heart, he kept on making up faces, and never uttered a word of complaint.

"He is a first-rate patient," said the surgeon as we passed along. "He keeps up good spirits all the time, and that helps all the rest."

In another part of the hospital was one of Birges's sharpshooters, who did such excellent service, you remember, at Fort Donelson. He was a brave and noble boy. There were several kind ladies taking care of the sick. Their presence was like sunshine. Wherever they walked the eyes of the sufferers followed them. One of these ladies thus speaks of little Frankie Bragg:—

"Many will remember him; the boy of fifteen, who fought valiantly at Donelson,—one of the bravest of Birges's sharpshooters, and whose answer to my questioning in regard to joining the army was so well worthy of record.

*" 'I joined, because I was so young and strong, and because life would be worth nothing to me unless I offered it for my country!'"*[26]

How noble! There are many strong men who have done nothing for their country, and there are some who enjoy all the blessings of a good government, who are willing to see it destroyed rather than lift a finger to save it. Their names shall go out in oblivion, but little Frankie Bragg shall live forever! His body lies in the hospital ground at Paducah, but the pure patriotism which animated him, and the words he uttered, will never die!

The good lady who took care of him writes:

I saw him die. I can never forget the pleading gaze of his violet eyes, the brow from which ringlets of light-brown hair were swept by strange fingers bathed in the death-dew, the desire for some one to care for him, some one to love him in his last hours. I came to his side, and he clasped my hand in his own, fast growing cold and stiff.

'O, I am going to die, and there is no one to love me,' he said. 'I did not think I was going to die till now; but it can't last long. If my sisters were only here; but I have no friends near me now, and it is so hard!'

'Frankie,' I said, 'I know it is hard to be away from your relatives, but you are not friendless; I am your friend. Mrs. S— and the kind Doctor are your friends, and we will all take care of you. More than this, God is your friend, and he is nearer to you now than either of us can get. Trust him, my boy. He will help you.'

A faint smile passed over the pale sufferer's features.

'O, do you think he will?' he asked.

Then, as he held my hands closer, he turned his face more fully toward me, and said: 'My mother taught me to pray when I was a very little boy, and I never forgot it. I have always said my prayers every day, and tried not to be bad. Do you think God heard me always?'

'Yes, most assuredly. Did he not promise, in his good Book, from which your mother taught you, that he would always hear the prayers of his children? Ask, and ye shall receive. Don't you remember this? One of the worst things we can do is to doubt God's truth. He has promised, and he will fulfil. Don't you feel so, Frankie?'

---

26: Hospital Incidents, *New York Post*, October 22, 1863.

He hesitated a moment, and then answered, slowly: 'Yes, I do believe it. I am not afraid to die, but I want somebody to love me.'

The old cry for love, the strong yearning for the sympathy of kindred hearts. It would not be put down.

'Frankie, I love you. Poor boy! you shall not be left alone. Is not this some comfort to you?'

'Do you love me? Will you stay with me, and not leave me?'

'I will not leave you. Be comforted, I will stay as long as you wish.'

I kissed the pale forehead as if it had been that of my own child. A glad light flashed over his face.

'O, kiss me again; that was given like my sister. Mrs. S—, won't you kiss me, too? I don't think it will be so hard to die, if you will both love me.'

It did not last long. With his face nestled against mine, and his large blue eyes fixed in perfect composure upon me to the last moment, he breathed out his life.

So he died for his country. He sleeps on the banks of the beautiful Ohio. Men labour hard for riches, honour, and fame, but few, when life is over, will leave a nobler record than this young Christian patriot.

# CHAPTER 12

# From Fort Pillow to Memphis

On the 6th of May, 1861, the Legislature of Tennessee, in secret session, voted that the State should secede from the Union. The next day, Governor Harris appointed three Commissioners to meet Mr. Hilliard, of Alabama, who had been sent by Jefferson Davis to make a league with the State. These Commissioners agreed that all the troops of the State should be under the control of the President of the Confederacy. All of the public property and naval stores and munitions of war were also turned over to the Confederacy. The people had nothing to do about it. The conspirators did not dare to trust the matter to them, for a great many persons in East Tennessee were ardently attached to the Union. In Western Tennessee, along the Mississippi, nearly all of the people, on the other hand, were in favour of secession.

At Memphis they were very wild and fierce. Union men were mobbed, tarred and feathered, ridden on rails, had their heads shaved, were robbed, knocked down, and warned to leave the place or be hung. One man was headed up in a hogshead, and rolled into the river, because he stood up for the Union! Memphis was a hotbed of secessionists; it was almost as bad as Charleston.

A Memphis newspaper, of the 6th of May, said:

Tennessee is disenthralled at last. Freedom has again crowned her with a fresh and fadeless wreath. She will do her entire duty. Great sacrifices are demanded of her, and they will be cheerfully made. Her blood and treasure are offered without stint at the shrine of Southern freedom. She counts not the cost at which independence may be bought. The gallant volunteer State of the South, her brave sons, now rushing to the standard of the Southern Confederacy, will sustain, by their unflinching valour and deathless devotion, her ancient renown achieved on so many battle-fields.

In fact, our entire people—men, women, and children—have engaged in this fight, and are animated by the single heroic and indomitable resolve to perish rather than submit to the despicable invader now threatening us with subjugation. They will ratify the ordinance of secession amid the smoke and carnage of battle; they will write out their endorsement of it with the blood of their foe; they will enforce it at the point of the bayonet and sword.

"Welcome, thrice welcome, glorious Tennessee, to the thriving family of Southern Confederate States![27]

On the same day the citizens of Memphis tore down the Stars and Stripes from its staff upon the Court-House, formed a procession, and with a band of music bore the flag, like a corpse, to a pit, and buried it in mock solemnity. They went into the public square, where stands the statue of General Jackson, and chiselled from its pedestal his memorable words: "The Federal Union,—it must be preserved." They went to the river-bank, and seized all the steamboats they could lay their hands upon belonging to Northern men.

They resolved to build a fleet of gunboats, which would ascend the river to St. Louis, Cincinnati, and Pittsburg, and compel the people of those cities to pay tribute, for the privilege of navigating the river to the Gulf.

The entire population engaged in the enterprise. The ladies held fairs and gave their jewellery. The citizens organized themselves into a gunboat association. When the boats were launched, the ladies, with appropriate ceremonies, dedicated them to the Confederacy. They urged their husbands, brothers, sons, and friends to enlist in the service, and the young man who hesitated received presents of hoopskirts, petticoats, and other articles of female wearing apparel.

Eight gunboats were built. Commodore Hollins, as you have seen, commanded them. He attempted to drive back General Pope at New Madrid, but failed. He went to New Orleans, and Captain Montgomery was placed in command.

When Commodore Foote and General Pope took Island No. 10, those that escaped of the Rebels fell back to Fort Pillow, about forty miles above Memphis. It was a strong position, and Commodore

---

27: *Memphis Avalanche.*

Foote made but little effort to take it, but waited for the advance of General Halleck's army upon Corinth. While thus waiting, one foggy morning, several of the Rebel gunboats made a sudden attack upon the *Cincinnati*, and nearly disabled her before they were beaten back. Meanwhile, Commodore Foote, finding that his wound, received at Donelson, was growing worse, was recalled by the Secretary of the Navy, and Commodore Charles Henry Davis, of Cambridge, Massachusetts, was placed in command.

Besides the gunboats on the Mississippi, was Colonel Ellet's fleet of rams,—nine in all. They were old steamboats, with oaken bulwarks three feet thick, to protect the boilers and engines. Their bows had been strengthened with stout timbers and iron bolts, and they had iron prows projecting under water. They carried no cannon, but were manned by sharpshooters. There were loop-holes through the timbers for the riflemen. The pilot-house was protected by iron plates. They joined the fleet at Fort Pillow.

The river is very narrow in front of the fort,—not more than a third of its usual width. It makes a sharp bend. The channel is deep, and the current rushes by like a mill-race. The Tennessee shore was lined with batteries on the bluff, which made it a place much stronger than Columbus or Island No. 10. But when General Beauregard was forced to evacuate Corinth, the Rebels were also compelled to leave Fort Pillow. For two or three days before the evacuation, they kept up a heavy fire upon the fleet.

On the 3rd of June,—a hot, sultry day,—just before night, a huge bank of clouds rolled up from the south. There had been hardly a breath of air through the day, but now the wind blew a hurricane. The air was filled with dust, whirled up from the sand-bars. When the storm was at its height, I was surprised to see two of the rams run down past the point of land which screened them from the batteries, vanishing from sight in the distant cloud. They went to ascertain what the Rebels were doing. There was a sudden waking up of heavy guns. The batteries were in a blaze. The cloud was thick and heavy, and the rams returned, but the Rebel cannon still thundered, throwing random shots into the river, two or three at a time, firing as if the Confederacy had tons of ammunition to spare.

The dust-cloud, with its fine, misty rain, rolled away. The sun shone once more, and bridged the river with a gorgeous arch of green and gold, which appeared a moment, and then faded away, as the sun went down behind the western woods. While we stood admiring the scene, a Rebel steamer came round the point to see what we were about. It was a black craft, bearing the flag of the Confederacy at her bow. She turned leisurely, stopped her wheels, and looked at us audaciously. The gunboats opened fire. The Rebel steamer took her own time, unmindful of the shot and shell falling and bursting all around her, then slowly disappeared beyond the headland. It was a challenge for a fight. It was not accepted, for Commodore Davis was not disposed to be cut up by the shore-batteries.

The next day there were lively times at the fort. A cannonade was kept up on Commodore Davis's fleet, which was vigorously answered. We little thought that this was to blind us to what was going on. At sunset the Rebels set fire to their barracks. There were great pillars of flame and smoke in and around the fort. The southern sky was all aglow. Occasionally there were flashes and explosions, sudden puffs of smoke, spreading out like flakes of cotton or fleeces of white and crimson wool. It was a gorgeous sight.

In the morning we found that the Rebels had gone, spiking their cannon and burning their supplies. That which had cost them months of hard labour was abandoned, and the river was open to Memphis.

On the 5th of June, Commodore Davis's fleet left Fort Pillow for Memphis. I was sitting at dinner with the Commodore and Captain Phelps, on board the *Benton*, when an orderly thrust his head into the cabin, and said, "Sir, there is a fine large steamer ahead of us."

We are on deck in an instant. The boatswain is piping all hands to quarters. There is great commotion.

"Out with that gun! Quick!" shouted Lieutenant Bishop. The brave tars seize the ropes, the trucks creak, and the great eleven-inch gun, already loaded, is out in a twinkling. Men are bringing up shot and shell. The deck is clearing of all superfluous furniture.

There she is, a mile distant, a beautiful steamer, head up-stream. She sees us, and turns her bow. Her broadside comes round, and we read "*Sovereign*" upon her wheelhouse. We are on the upper deck, and the muzzle of the eleven-inch gun is immediately beneath us. A great flash comes in our faces. We are in a cloud, stifled, stunned, gasping for breath, our ears ringing; but the cloud is blown away, and we see the shot throw up the water a mile beyond the *Sovereign*. Glorious! We will have her. Another, not so good. Another, still worse.

The *Louisville*, *Carondelet*, and *Cairo* open fire. But the *Sovereign* is a fast sailer, and is increasing the distance.

"The *Spitfire* will catch her!" says the pilot. A wave of the hand, and the Spitfire is alongside, running up like a dog to its master. Lieutenant Bishop, Pilot Bixby, and a gun crew jump on board the tug, which carries a boat howitzer. Away they go, the tug puffing and wheezing, as if it had the asthma.

"Through the *chute*!" shouts Captain Phelps.

*Chute* is a French word, meaning a narrow passage, not the main channel of the river. The Sovereign is in the main channel, but the *Spitfire* has the shortest distance. The tug cuts the water like a knife. She comes out just astern of the steamer. *Bang!* goes the howitzer. The shot falls short. *Bang!* again in a twinkling. Better. *Bang!* It goes over the *Sovereign*.

"Hurrah! Bishop will get her!" The crews of the gunboats dance with delight, and swing their caps. *Bang!* Right through her cabin. The *Sovereign* turns towards the shore, and runs plump against the bank. The crew, all but the cook, take to the woods, and the steamer is ours. It would astonish you to see how fast a well-drilled boat's-crew can load and fire a howitzer. Commodore Foote informed me that, when he was in the China Sea, he was attacked by the natives, and his boat's-crew fired four times a minute!

The chase for the *Sovereign* was very exciting,—more so than any horse-race I ever saw. The crew on board the *Sovereign* had been stopping at all the farm-houses along the river, setting fire to the cotton on the plantations. They did it in the name of the Confederate government, that it might not fall into the hands of the Yankees. In a great many places they had rolled it into the river, and the stream was covered with white flakes. The bushes were lined with it. As soon as the people along the banks saw the Federal steamboats, they went to work to save their property. Some of them professed to be Union men. I conversed with an old man, who was lame, and could hardly hobble round. He spoke bitterly against Jeff Davis for burning his cotton and stealing all his property.

While descending the river, we saw a canoe, containing two men, push out from a thick canebrake. They came up to the *Benton*. We thought they were Rebels, at first, but soon saw they were two pilots belonging to the fleet, who had started the day before for Vicksburg, to pilot Commodore Farragut's fleet to Memphis. They had been concealed during the day, not daring to move. The evacuation of Fort Pillow rendered it unnecessary for them to continue the voyage. They said that eight Rebel gunboats were a short distance below us. We moved on slowly, and came to anchor about nine o'clock, near a place called by all the rivermen Paddy's Hen and Chickens, about two miles above Memphis.

# CHAPTER 13

# The Naval Fight at Memphis

On the evening of the 5th of June, while we were lying above Memphis, Commodore Montgomery, commanding the fleet of Rebel gunboats built by the citizens and ladies of Memphis, was making a speech in the Gayoso Hall of that city. There was great excitement. It was known at noon that Fort Pillow was evacuated. The stores were immediately closed. Some people commenced packing up their goods to leave,— expecting that the city would be burned if the Yankees obtained possession. Commodore Montgomery said: "I have no intention of retreating any farther. I have come here, that you may see Lincoln's gunboats sent to the bottom by the fleet which you built and manned."

The rabble cheered him, and believed his words. On the morning of the 6th, one of the newspapers assured the people that the Federal fleet would not reach the city. It said:

> All obstructions to their progress are not yet removed, and probably will not be. The prospect is very good for a grand naval engagement which shall eclipse anything ever seen before. There are many who would like the engagement to occur, who do not much relish the prospect of its occurring very near the city. They think deeper water and scope and verge enough for such an encounter may be found farther up the river. All, however, are rejoiced to learn that Memphis will not fall till conclusions are first tried on water, and at the cannon's mouth.[28]

I was awake early enough to see the brightening of the morning. Never was there a lovelier daybreak. The woods were full of songbirds. The air was balmy. A few light clouds, fringed with gold, lay along the eastern horizon.

---

28: *Memphis Avalanche,* June 6, 1862.

The fleet of five gunboats was anchored in a line across the river. The *Benton* was nearest the Tennessee shore, next was the *Carondelet*, then the *Louisville*, *St. Louis*, and, lastly, the *Cairo*. Near by the *Cairo*, tied up to the Arkansas shore, were the *Queen City* and the *Monarch*,—two of Colonel Ellet's rams. The tugs *Jessie Benton* and *Spitfire* hovered near the *Benton*, Commodore Davis's flag-ship. It was their place to be within call, to carry orders to the other boats of the fleet.

Before sunrise the anchors were up, and the boats kept their position in the stream by the slow working of the engines.

Commodore Davis waved his hand, and the Jessie *Benton* was alongside the flag-ship in a moment.

"Drop down towards the city, and see if you can discover the Rebel fleet," was the order.

I jumped on board the tug. Below us was the city. The first rays of the sun were gilding the church-spires. A crowd of people stood upon the broad levee between the city and the river. They were coming from all the streets, on foot, on horseback, in carriages,— men, women, and children—ten thousand, to see Lincoln's gunboats sent to the bottom. Above the court-house, and from flagstaffs, waved the flag of the Confederacy. A half-dozen river steamers lay at the landing, but the Rebel fleet was not in sight. At our right hand was the wide marsh on the tongue of land where Wolfe River empties into the Mississippi. Upon our left were the cotton-trees and button-woods, and the village of Hopedale at the terminus of the Little Rock and Memphis Railroad. We dropped slowly down the stream, the tug floating in the swift current, running deep and strong as it sweeps past the city.

The crowd increased. The levee was black with the multitude. The windows were filled. The flat roofs of the warehouses were covered with the excited throng, which surged to and fro as we upon the tug came down into the bend, almost within talking distance.

Suddenly a boat came out from the Arkansas shore, where it had been lying concealed from view behind the forest,—another, another, eight of them. They formed in two lines, in front of the city.

Nearest the city, in the front line, was the *General Beauregard*; next, the *Little Rebel*; then the *General Price* and the *Sumter*. In the second line, behind the *Beauregard*, was the *General Lovell*; behind the *Little Rebel* was the *Jeff Thompson*; behind the *General Price* was the *General Bragg*; and behind the *Sumter* was the Van Dorn.

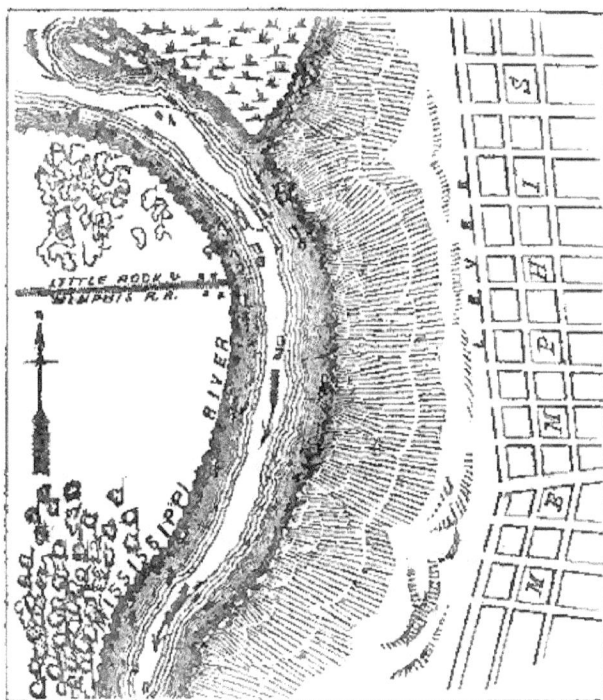

NAVAL FIGHT AT MEMPHIS, June 6, 1862.

1 Federal Gunboats.
2, 2 General Beauregard.
3, 3 Little Rebel.
4, 4 General Price.
5, 5 Sumter.
6, 6 General Lovell.

7, 7 General Thompson.
8, 8 General Bragg.
9, 9 General Van Dorn.
Q Queen City.
M Monarch.

These boats were armed as follows: *General Beauregard*, 4 guns *Little Rebel* (flag-ship), 2 *General Price*, 4 *Sumter*, 3 *General Lovell*, 4 *General Thompson*, 4 *General Bragg*, 3 *General Van Dorn*, 4—Total, 28.

The guns were nearly all rifled, and were of long range. They were pivoted, and could be whirled in all directions. The boilers of the boats were casemated and protected by iron plates, but the guns were exposed. The accompanying diagram will show you the position of both fleets at the beginning and at the close of the engagement.

Slowly and steadily they came into line. The *Little Rebel* moved through the fleet, and Commodore Montgomery issued his orders to each captain in person. The *Benton* and *St. Louis* dropped down towards the city, to protect the tug. A signal brought us back, and the boats moved up-stream again, to the original position.

There was another signal from the flag-ship, and then on board all the boats there was a shrill whistle. It was the boatswain piping all hands to quarters. The drummer beat his roll, and the marines seized their muskets. The sailors threw open the ports, ran out the guns, brought up shot and shells, stowed away furniture, took down rammers and sponges, seized their handspikes, stripped off their coats, rolled up their sleeves, loaded the cannon, and stood by their pieces. Cutlasses and boarding-pikes were distributed. Last words were said. They waited for orders.

"Let the men have their breakfasts," was the order from the flag-ship.

Commodore Davis believed in fighting on full stomachs. Hot coffee, bread, and beef were carried round to the men.

The Rebel fleet watched us awhile. The crowd upon the shore increased. Perhaps they thought the Yankees did not dare to fight. At length the Rebel fleet began to move up-stream.

"Round to; head down-stream; keep in line with the flag-ship," was the order which we on board the *Jessie Benton* carried to each boat of the line. We returned, and took our position between the *Benton* and *Carondelet*.

I stood on the top of the tug, beside the pilot-house. Stand with me there, and behold the scene. The sun is an hour high, and its bright rays lie in a broad line of silver light upon the eddying stream. You look down the river to the city, and behold the housetops, the windows, the levee, crowded with men, women, and children. The flag of the Confederacy floats defiantly. The Rebel fleet is moving slowly towards us. A dense cloud of smoke rolls up from the chimneys of the steamers, and floats over the city.

There is a flash, a puff from the *Little Rebel*, a sound of something unseen in the air, and a column of water is thrown up a mile behind us. A second shot, from the *Beauregard*, falls beside the *Benton*. A third, from the *Price*, aimed at the *Carondelet*, misses by a foot or two, and dashes up the water between the *Jessie Benton* and the flag-ship. It is a sixty-four-pounder. If it had struck us, our boat would have been splintered to kindlings in an instant.

Commodore Montgomery sees that the boats of the Federal fleet have their iron-plated bows up-stream. He comes up rapidly, to crush them at the stern, where there are no iron plates. A signal goes up from the *Benton*, and the broadsides begin to turn towards the enemy. The crowd upon the levee think that the Federal boats are retreating, and hurrah for Commodore Montgomery.

There has been profound silence on board the Union gunboats. The men are waiting for the word. It comes.

"Open fire, and take close quarters."

The *Cairo* begins. A ten-inch shot screams through the air, and skips along the water towards the *Little Rebel*. Another, from the *St. Louis*. A third, from the *Louisville*. Another, from the *Carondelet*, and lastly, from the *Benton*. The gunners crouch beside their guns, to track the shot. Some are too high, some too low. There is an answering roar from all the Rebel boats. The air is full of indescribable noises. The water boils and bubbles around us. It is tossed up in columns and jets. There are sudden flashes overhead, explosions, and sulphurous clouds, and whirring of ragged pieces of iron. The uproar increases. The cannonade reverberates from the high bluff behind the city to the dark-green forest upon the Arkansas shore, and echoes from bend to bend.

The space between the fleets is gradually lessening. The Yankees are not retreating, but advancing. A shot strikes the *Little Rebel*. One tears through the *General Price*. Another through the *General Bragg*. Commodore Montgomery is above the city, and begins to fall back. He is not ready to come to close quarters. Fifteen minutes pass by, but it seems not more than two. How fast one lives at such a time! All of your senses are quickened. You see everything, hear everything. The blood rushes through your veins. Your pulse is quickened. You long to get at the enemy,—to sweep over the intervening space, lay your boat alongside, pour in a broadside, and knock them to pieces in a twinkling! You care nothing for the screaming of the shot, the bursting of the shells. You have got over all that. You have but one thought,—*to tear down that hateful flaunting flag, to smite the enemies of your country into the dust!*

While this cannonade was going on, I noticed the two rams casting loose from the shore. I heard the tinkle of the engineer's bell for more fire and a full head of steam. The sharpshooters took their places. The *Queen* came out from the shelter of the great cottonwoods, crossed the river, and passed down between the *Benton* and *Carondelet*. Colonel Ellet stood beside the pilot, and waved his hand to us on board the *Jessie Benton*. The *Monarch* was a little later, and, instead of following in the wake of the *Queen*, passed between the *Cairo* and the *St. Louis*.

See the *Queen*! Her great wheels whirl up clouds of spray, and leave a foaming path. She carries a silver train sparkling in the morning light. She ploughs a furrow, which rolls the width of the river. Our boat dances like a feather on the waves. She gains the intervening space between the fleets. Never moved a Queen so determinedly, never one more fleet,—almost leaping from the water. The Stars and Stripes stream to the breeze beneath the black banner unfolding, expanding, and trailing far away from her smoke-stacks. There is a surging, hissing, and smothered screaming of the pent-up steam in her boilers, as if they had put on all energy for the moment. They had;—flesh, blood, bones, iron, brass, steel,—animate and inanimate,—were nerved up for the trial of the hour!

Officers and men behold her in astonishment and admiration. For a moment there is silence. The men stand transfixed by their guns, forgetting their duties. Then the Rebel gunners, as if moved by a common impulse, bring their guns to bear upon her. She is exposed on the right, on the left, and in front. It is a terrible cross-fire. Solid shot scream past. Shells explode around her. She is pierced through and through. Her timbers crack. She quivers beneath the shock, but does not falter. On—on—faster—straight towards the *General Beauregard*.

The commander of that vessel adroitly avoids the stroke. The *Queen* misses her aim. She sweeps by like a race-horse, receiving the fire of the *Beauregard* on one side and the *Little Rebel* on the other. She comes round in a graceful curve, almost lying down upon her side, as if to cool her heated smoke-stacks in the stream. The stern guns of the *Beauregard* send their shot through the bulwarks of the *Queen*. A splinter strikes the brave commander, Colonel Ellet. He is knocked down, bruised, and stunned for a moment, but springs to his feet, steadies himself against the pilot-house, and gives his directions as coolly as if nothing had happened.

The *Queen* passes round the *Little Rebel*, and approaches the *General Price*.

"Take her aft the wheelhouse," says Colonel Ellet to the pilot. The commander of the *Price* turns towards the approaching antagonist. Her wheels turn. She surges ahead to escape the terrible blow. Too late. There is a splintering, crackling, crashing of timbers. The broadside of the boat is crushed in. It is no more than a box of cards or thin tissue-paper before the terrible blow.

There are jets of flame and smoke from the loop-holes of the *Queen*. The sharpshooters are at it. You hear the rattling fire, and see the crew of the *Price* running wildly over the deck, tossing their arms. The unceasing thunder of the cannonade drowns their cries. A moment, and a white flag goes up. The *Price* surrenders.

But the *Queen* has another antagonist, the *Beauregard*. The *Queen* is motionless, but the *Beauregard* sweeps down with all her powers. There is another crash. The bulwarks of the *Queen* tremble before the stroke. There is a great opening in her hull. But no white flag is displayed. There are no cries for quarter, no thoughts of surrendering. The sharpshooters pick off the gunners of the *Beauregard*, compelling them to take shelter beneath their casemates.

We who see it hold our breaths. We are unmindful of the explosions around us. How will it end? Will the *Queen* sink with all her brave men on board?

But her consort is at hand, the *Monarch*, commanded by Captain Ellet, brother of Colonel Ellet. He was five or ten minutes behind the *Queen* in starting, but he has appeared at the right moment. He, too, has been unmindful of the shot and shell falling around him. He aims straight as an arrow for the *Beauregard*. The *Beauregard* is stiff, stanch, and strong, but her timbers, planks, knees, and braces are no more than laths before the powerful stroke of the *Monarch*. The sharpshooters pour in their fire. The engineer of the *Monarch* puts his force-pumps in play and drenches the decks of the *Beauregard* with scalding water. An officer of the *Beauregard* raises a white cloth upon a rammer. It is a signal for surrender. The sharpshooters stop firing. There are the four boats, three of them floating helplessly in the stream, the water pouring into the hulls, through the splintered planking.

Captain Ellet saw that the *Queen* was disabled, and took her in tow to the Arkansas shore. Prompted by humanity, instead of falling upon the other vessels of the fleet he took the *General Price* to the shore.

The *Little Rebel* was pierced through her hull by a half-dozen shots. Commodore Montgomery saw that the day was lost. He ran alongside the *Beauregard*, and, notwithstanding the vessel had surrendered, took the crew on board, to escape. But a shot from the *Cairo* passed through the boilers. The steam rushed out like the hissing of serpents. The boat was near the shore, and the crew jumped into the water, climbed the bank, and fled to the woods. The *Cairo* gave them a broadside of shells as they ran.

The *Beauregard* was fast settling. The *Jessie Benton* ran alongside. All had fled save the wounded. There was a pool of blood upon the deck. The sides of the casemate were stained with crimson drops, yet warm from the heart of a man who had been killed by a shell.

"Help, quick!" was the cry of Captain Maynadier.

We rushed on board in season to save a wounded officer. The vessel settled slowly to the bottom.

173

"I thank you," said the officer, "for saving me from drowning. You are my enemies, but you have been kinder to me than those whom I called my friends. One of my brother officers when he fled, had the meanness to pick my pocket and steal my watch!"

Thus those who begun by stealing public property, forts, and arsenals, did not hesitate to violate their honour,—fleeing after surrendering, forsaking their wounded comrade, robbing him of his valuables, and leaving him to drown!

There is no cessation of the cannonade. The fight goes on. The *Benton* is engaged with the *General Lovell*. They are but a few rods apart, and both within a stone's-throw of the multitude upon the shore.

Captain Phelps stands by one of the *Benton's* rifled guns. He waits to give a raking shot, runs his eye along the sights, and gives the word to fire. The steel-pointed shot enters the starboard side of the hull, by the water-line. Timbers, braces, planks, the whole side of the boat seemingly, are torn out.

The water pours in. The vessel settles to the guards, to the ports, to the top of the casemate, reels, and with a lurch disappears. It is the work of three minutes.

The current sets swiftly along the shore. The plummet gives seventy-five feet of water. The vessel goes down like a lump of lead. Her terror-stricken crew are thrown into the current. It is an appalling sight. A man with his left arm torn, broken, bleeding, and dangling by his side, runs wildly over the deck. There is unspeakable horror in his face. He beckons now to those on shore, and now to his friends on board the boats. He looks imploringly to heaven, and calls for help. Unavailing the cry. He disappears in the eddying whirlpool. A hundred human beings are struggling for life, buffeting the current, raising their arms, catching at sticks, straws, planks, and timbers. *"Help! help! help!"* they cry. It is a wild wail of agony, mingled with the cannonade.

There is no help for them on shore. There, within a dozen rods, are their friends, their fathers, mothers, brothers, sisters, wives, children, they who urged them to join the service, who compelled them to enlist. All are powerless to aid them!

They who stand upon the shore behold those whom they love defeated, crushed, drowning, calling for help! It is an hour when heart-strings are wrung. Tears, cries, prayers, efforts, all are unavailing.

Commodore Davis beholds them. His heart is touched. "Save them, lads," he says.

The crews of the *Benton* and *Carondelet* rush to their boats. So eager are they to save the struggling men that one of the boats is swamped in the launching. Away they go, picking up one here, another there,—ten or twelve in all. A few reach the shore and are helped up the bank by lookers-on; but fifty or sixty sink to rise no more. How noble the act! How glorious! Bright amid all the distress, all the horror, all the infamous conduct of men who have forsworn themselves, will shine forever, like a star of heaven, this act of humanity!

The *General Price*, *General Beauregard*, *Little Rebel*, and *General Lovell*—one half of the Rebel fleet—were disposed of. The other vessels attempted to flee. The Union fleet had swept steadily on in an unbroken line. Amid all the appalling scenes of the hour there was no lull in the cannonade. While saving those who had lost all power of resistance, there was no cessation of effort to crush those who still resisted.

A short distance below the *Little Rebel*, the *Jeff Thompson*, riddled by shot, and in flames, was run ashore. A little farther down-stream the *General Bragg* was abandoned, also in flames from the explosion of a nine-inch shell, thrown by the *St. Louis*. The crews leaped on shore, and fled to the woods. The *Sumter* went ashore, near the *Little Rebel*. The *Van Dorn* alone escaped. She was a swift steamer, and was soon beyond reach of the guns of the fleet.

The fight is over. The thunder of the morning dies away, and the birds renew their singing. The abandoned boats are picked up. The *Jeff Thompson* cannot be saved. The flames leap around the chimneys. The boilers are heated to redness. A pillar of fire springs upward, in long lances of light. The interior of the boat—boilers, beams of iron, burning planks, flaming timbers, cannon-shot, shells—is lifted five hundred feet in air, in an expanding, unfolding cloud, filled with loud explosions. The scattered fragments rain upon forest, field, and river, as if meteors of vast proportions had fallen from heaven to earth, taking fire in their descent. There is a shock which shakes all Memphis, and announces to the disappointed, terror-stricken, weeping, humiliated multitude that the drama which they have played so madly for a twelvemonth is over, that retribution for crime has come at last!

Thus in an hour's time the Rebel fleet was annihilated. Commodore Montgomery was to have sent the Union boats to the bottom; but his expectations were not realized, his promises not fulfilled. It is not known how many men were lost on the Rebel side, but probably from eighty to a hundred. Colonel Ellet was the only one injured on board the Union fleet. The gunboats were uninjured. The *Queen of the West* was the only boat disabled. In striking contrast was the damage to Montgomery's fleet:

Sunk, *General Price*, 4 guns. *General Beauregard*, 4; *General Lovell*, 4
Burned, *Jeff Thompson*, 4;
Captured, *General Bragg*, 3; *Sumter*, 3; *Little Rebel*, 2—24

The bow guns of Commodore Davis's fleet only were used in the attack, making sixteen guns in all brought to bear upon the Rebel fleet. The *Cairo* and *St. Louis* fired broadsides upon the crews as they fled to the woods.

********

The retreating of the Rebel fleet carried the Union gunboats several miles below the city before the contest was over. At ten o'clock Commodore Davis steamed back to the city. There stood the multitude, confounded by what had taken place. A boat came off from the shore, pulled by two oarsmen, and bringing a citizen, Dr. Dickerson, who waved a white handkerchief. He was a messenger from the Mayor, tendering the surrender of the city. There were some men in the crowd who shook their fists at us, and cried, "O you blue-bellied Yankees! You devils! You scoundrels!" We could bear it very well, after the events of the morning. A few hurrahed for Jeff Davis, but the multitude made no demonstration.

A regiment landed, and marched up Monroe Street to the courthouse. I had the pleasure of accompanying the soldiers. The band played Yankee Doodle and Hail Columbia. How proudly the soldiers marched! They halted in front of the court-house. An officer went to the top of the building, tore down the Rebel flag, and flung out the Stars and Stripes.

Wild and hearty were the cheers of the troops. The buried flag had risen from its grave, to wave forevermore,—the emblem of power, justice, liberty, and law!

Thus the Upper Mississippi was opened again to trade and the peaceful pursuits of commerce. How wonderfully it was repossessed. The fleet lost not a man at Island No. 10, not a man at New Madrid, not a man at Fort Pillow, not a man at Memphis, by the fire of the Rebels! How often had we been told that the strongholds of the Rebels were impregnable! How often that the Union gunboats would be blown up by torpedoes, or sent to the bottom by the batteries or by the Rebel fleet! How often that the river would never be opened till

176

the Confederacy was recognized as an independent power! General Butler was in possession of New Orleans, Memphis was held by Commodore Davis, and the mighty river was all but open through its entire length to trade and navigation. In one year this was accomplished. So moves a nation in a career unparalleled in history, rescuing from the grasp of pirates and plunderers the garnered wealth of centuries.

In 1861, when Tennessee seceded, the steamer *Platte Valley*, owned in *St. Louis*, belonging to the St. Louis and Memphis Steamboat Company, was the last boat permitted to leave for the North. All others were stolen by the secessionists, who repudiated the debts they owed Northern men. The *Platte Valley*, commanded by Captain Wilcox, was in Commodore Davis's fleet of transports. Captain Wilcox recognized some of his old acquaintances in the crowd, and informed them that in a day or two he would resume his regular trips between St. Louis and Memphis! They were ready to send up cargoes of sugar and cotton. So trade accompanies the flag of our country wherever it goes.

This narrative which I have given you is very tame. Look at the scene once more,—the early morning, the cloudless sky, the majestic river, the hostile fleets, the black pall of smoke overhanging the city, the forest, the stream, the moving of the boats, the terrific cannonade, the assembled thousands, the glorious advance of the *Queen* and the *Monarch*, the crashing and splintering of timbers, the rifle-shots, the sinking of vessels, the cries of drowning men, the gallantry of the crews of the *Benton* and *Carondelet*, the weeping and wailing of the multitude, the burnings, the explosions, the earthquake shock, which shakes the city to its foundations! These are the events of a single hour. Remember the circumstances,—that the fight is before the city, before expectant thousands, who have been invited to the entertainment,—the sinking of the Union fleet,—that they are to see the prowess of their husbands, brothers, and friends, that their strength is utter weakness,—that, after thirteen months of robbery, outrage, and villainy, the despised, insulted flag of the Union rises from its burial, and waves once more above them in stainless purity and glory! Take all under consideration, if you would feel the moral sublimity of the hour!

In these pages I have endeavoured to make a contribution of facts to the history of this great struggle of our beloved country for national life.

www.ingramcontent.com/pod-product-compliance
Lightning Source LLC
Chambersburg PA
CBHW021103090426
42738CB00006B/482